A WAR OF WORDS
POLITICAL VIOLENCE AND
PUBLIC DEBATE IN ISRAEL

Cass Series: Political Violence
Series Editors: Paul Wilkinson and David Rapoport

Terrorism versus Democracy: The Liberal State Response
Paul Wilkinson

Aviation Terrorism and Security
Paul Wilkinson and Brian M. Jenkins (eds)

Counter-Terrorist Law and Emergency Powers in the United Kingdom, 1922–2000
Laura K. Donohue

The Democratic Experience and Political Violence
David C. Rapoport and Leonard Weinberg (eds)

Inside Terrorist Organizations
David C. Rapoport (ed.)

The Future of Terrorism
Max Taylor and John Horgan (eds)

Globalisation and the Future of Terrorism
Brynjar Lia and Annika S. Hansen (eds)

The IRA, 1968–2000: An Analysis of a Secret Army
J. Bowyer Bell

Millennial Violence: Past, Present and Future
Jeffrey Kaplan (ed.)

Right-Wing Extremism in the Twenty-First Century
Peter H. Merkl and Leonard Weinberg (eds)

Terrorism Today
Christopher C. Harmon

The Psychology of Terrorism
John Horgan and Max Taylor (eds)

Research on Terrorism: Trends, Achievements and Failures
Andrew Silke (ed.)

A War of Words: Political Violence and Public Debate in Israel
Gerald Cromer

A WAR OF WORDS

POLITICAL VIOLENCE AND PUBLIC DEBATE IN ISRAEL

GERALD CROMER
Bar Ilan University

LONDON AND NEW YORK

First published 2004 by FRANK CASS PUBLISHERS.

This edition published 2014 by
ROUTLEDGE
4 Park Square, Milton Park, Abingdon, Oxon OX14 4RN
605 Third Avenue, New York, NY 10017

*Routledge is an imprint of the Taylor & Francis Group,
an informa business*

Copyright © 2004 Gerald Cromer

All rights reserved. No part of this book may be reprinted or reproduced or utilised in any form or by any electronic, mechanical, or other means, now known or hereafter invented, including photocopying and recording, or in any information storage or retrieval system, without permission in writing from the publishers.

Notice:
Product or corporate names may be trademarks or registered trademarks and are used only for identification and explanation without intent to infringe.

British Library Cataloguing in Publication Data
A catalogue record for this book is available
from the British Library

ISBN 13: 978-0-7146-5631-1 (hbk)
ISBN 13: 978-0-7146-8516-8 (pbk)

Library of Congress Cataloging-in-Publication Data

Cromer, Gerald, 1944–
  A war of words: political violence and public debate in Israel / Gerald Cromer.
    p. cm.
  Includes bibliographical references and index.
  1. Political violence–Israel–Public opinion. 2. Arab–Israeli conflict–Public opinion. 3. Public opinion–Israel. 4. Terrorism–Government policy–Israel. 5. Israel–Politics and government. 6. Political culture–Israel. I. Title.

HN660.Z9V53 2004
303.6'095694–dc22

2003065599

Typeset in 11/13pt Classical Garamond by Vitaset, Paddock Wood, Kent

For the next generation,
Mayan, Ariel and Yael, Elisha and Tzahala, and Adam,
and the one after, Tuvia.

'Peace be within thy walls and tranquillity
within thy palaces.'

Psalms 122:7

Contents

List of Abbreviations ix

List of Illustrations x

Foreword xi

1: Introduction 1

2: The Body Politic 14

3: Terrorism 26

4: War 44

5: Verbal Violence 63

6: Racism 89

7: Remembering Violence 106

Conclusions 128

Bibliography 137

Index 147

Abbreviations

DMC	Democratic Movement for Change
FLN	*Front de la Liberation Nationale*/National Liberation Front
IDF	Israel Defence Forces
IRA	Irish Republican Army
MK	Member of Knesset
NRP	National Religious Party
PLO	Palestine Liberation Organisation
UNIFIL	United Nations Interim Force in Lebanon

Illustrations

1 Davar cartoon depicting the Likud as savages.   67

2 An Alignment election advertising poster using the settlement map as a motif in its critique of Menachem Begin's demagoguery.   78

3 An election campaign advertising poster illustrating the choice between Beginism and an enlightened government.   79

Foreword

Gerald Cromer has produced a fascinating, important and unusual book; one that will influence how those who study politics and those interested in violence will do their work. The editors of the series are delighted to have the volume and it comes at a particularly appropriate time.

Violence has influenced Jewish history and traditions enormously; perhaps no nation has experienced as many traumatic experiences over so long a period of time. Most often, others have attacked Jews; but Jews have assaulted other Jews, and of course, other peoples as well. In all three cases, the Jewish community has been seriously affected and its sense of identity reshaped.

Cromer examines how the participants in a political system understand violence, and how different recollections of the causes and consequences of crucial historical experiences compel them to cope with the present and prepare for the future. Israel is a particularly fruitful and engrossing context for studies of this kind, and that may help explain why the first study of this sort originates there.

Cromer's analysis is limited to a brief but particularly memorable period from 1977 to 1984. Egypt and Israel made peace; a peace that for very different reasons provoked different parties: the PLO, some Arab states and some Israeli religious elements. The Israelis invaded Lebanon ostensibly to destroy the PLO, which was then in the process of assembling a considerable military force of perhaps 25,000. The PLO was not destroyed, but it fled Lebanon greatly diminished; and eventually the Israelis were compelled to leave too as Israel became seared by what Americans would call a 'Vietnam Paradigm' or trauma.

All issues were complicated by the fact that for the first time a new party governed Israel – the Likud, led by Menachem Begin. The Likud had been on the 'periphery' of the Israeli political scene for 30 years, but was now revitalized by the influx of Jews expelled from various states in the Middle East and North Africa. Labour interpreted Begin's activities as an effort to realize the ultimate object of the terrorist campaign he led prior to independence. The religious Right saw the situation in a radically different way, namely that Begin deliberately betrayed his earlier vision, because the peace with Egypt created an enormous unnecessary obstacle to recovering all of the biblical lands. Beyond all this, the 1982 elections provoked a variety of violent assaults against the facilities and members of the Labour party, including one death from a grenade attack. Many Israelis believed that the fiery political language that the Likud used provoked those assaults, and the events were interpreted in the light of parallel incidents before independence.

In the battle for independence, the Zionist revisionists – represented by the Irgun (Begin's group) and the Lehi (an offshoot that the British called the 'Stern Gang') – challenged the Zionist Establishment. The charge was that the Establishment was too timid to push (i.e. fight) for independence, and eager to accept partition of the Holy Land, making it impossible to realize the original Zionist dream. The Establishment saw the violence of the revisionists as reckless and dangerous. Independence was achieved in spite of revisionist tactics not because of them.

After Israel was established (1948), the revisionists participated in parliamentary politics, but their earlier behavior made them a virtually illegal party. When the Likud moved to the 'center' of Israeli life, it attempted to correct the nation's historical memory in a variety of ways, i.e. with ceremonies to honor the revisionist veterans, attempts to re-examine responsibility for various violent instances between the two major elements of the Israeli political scene, etc.

Cromer exquisitely details how different recollections of Jewish and Israeli history shaped the ability of various elements of the public to cope with the Lebanon War and with Palestinian and Jewish religious terror. For the Israeli public the rebellions against Rome, particularly Bar Kochba's, which led to the loss of the Holy Land and the Exile, were re-examined for 'lessons' about the contemporary scene. Labor saw those rebellions as disasters produced by recklessness; the Likud understood them as being necessary to preserve Jewish identity, an essential part of which was an everlasting commitment to the Land. Labor saw the Holocaust as a unique event, one that could only happen in Exile, while the Likud argued that Arafat shared Hitler's purpose and the Holocaust's true meaning was that Israel too could become a victim of Jewish passivity.

The Jewish obsession with the violent past seems to be an unusual political experience, but Cromer argues that the experiences can teach us something about ourselves too. I think he must be right, for the simple and obvious reason that the State and violence are inseparable.

Americans tend to be oblivious to their past, but recollections are important as the continuing significance of the 'Vietnam Paradigm', for example, shows. The first Gulf War supposedly 'liberated' Americans from the trauma. But many were disappointed to see Saddam Hussein survive and thought that memories of Vietnam made the US terminate the war too soon. Certainly, Vietnam does help explain why the next administration in Washington displayed a reluctance to cope with Islamic terrorist attacks against the US military.

The attacks of 11 September 2001 seemed to eliminate the Vietnam Paradigm altogether. To many that sad day provided the first clear justification for a war of self-defense since Pearl Harbor. But it does seem that the 'shock and awe' invasion method was conceived to avoid potential problems associated with Vietnam. Furthermore, at the end of the day, Americans may discover that they are still significantly shaped by this earlier experience and unable to distinguish clearly between the different crucial ingredients of the two situations.

Vietnam was obviously not the first war to influence a future generation. Ironically, the US got into Vietnam partly because the Government was inspired by recollections that the appeasement policies of the 1930s had brought about World War II.

Contemporary American politics does not provide a clear example of a violent movement against the Establishment moving from the periphery to the center, though clearly Bill Clinton's unusual relationship toward the Vietnam War affected crucial decisions regarding the use of force when he became Commander-in-Chief.

But, if we broaden the historical horizons, we will find that a movement from periphery to center is not altogether foreign to American experiences. The Civil Rights Movement was, in a very important sense, a major step in ending Civil War controversies in American political life. But the leaders of the movement did not anticipate some of the consequences and ironies produced. After a century, the South was brought back into the political system in the sense that Southern politicians could now run for the presidency, and Americans have elected half of their presidents from the South since then – more than from any section of the country. A second unintended result was that the South became receptive to the Republican Party.

The flag of the Confederacy remains a source of annoyance to many Americans, and controversies over its display still beset the legal system and have influenced local and state elections in the South. Most recently (November 2003), Howard Dean, the leading contender for the Democratic presidential nomination, was forced to make profuse apologies for gratuitous comments about welcoming people with Confederate flags to his campaign; comments that might yet produce serious political consequences. These observations about recollections of three wars may tell us something important about the American political scene, but we need our Cromer to put them together systematically.

David Rapoport
2003

1

Introduction

NON-STATE VIOLENCE

In his classic essay on politics as a vocation, Max Weber argued that the state cannot be defined in terms of its ends; it can only be distinguished from other associations on the basis of the unique means used to achieve them. 'A state', he concluded,

> is a human community that (successfully) claims the *monopoly of the legitimate use of physical force* within a given territory... the right to use physical force is ascribed to other institutions or to individuals only to the extent to which the state permits it. The state is considered the sole source of the 'right' to use violence.[1]

For a long period of time this state-centred paradigm constituted the only school of thought in criminology. Theoreticians and field researchers alike restricted their attention to the political and conventional violence of non-state actors. The state use of force was considered legitimate and therefore irrelevant. Only with the advent of critical criminology in the 1970s did it become an issue of concern, and a topic considered worthy of academic research.

Weber seems to have had an even more long-lasting influence on those involved in the study of the response to crime and deviance. Since the 1960s social constructionists have tried to research the intricacies of the labelling process. However, controversies regarding the state use of force have gone largely unnoticed. Scholars have concentrated their attention instead on the polemic about non-state actors who resort to violence, and particularly on those who claim to do so for ideological reasons. They have been intrigued by dissenters whose violent actions are denuded of the political meaning they attribute to them. Thus, numerous studies show how political deviants are delegitimated on the grounds that they have criminal motives or no motives whatsoever.

The criminalization of non-state political violence takes one of two forms. In some instances, the perpetrators are accused of using ideological rhetoric as a cover for economic offences; in others their crimes are thought to be of an expressive rather than an instrumental nature. The resort to violence is portrayed as letting off steam. In both cases though, those concerned are exploiting the situation in order to engage in illegal acts. They are not really fighting for a cause.[2]

Dissidents are also depoliticized on the grounds that their violent actions derive from some kind of mental derangement. This is due to the fact that

> the sovereign cannot believe that anybody with a sane mind would rebel against his moral tenets. Everything is so good and promising in the society ... that only mentally abnormal individuals could oppose it, and only pathologically minded persons would commit political crimes.[3]

However, as Jock Young has pointed out, it is difficult to use the medical analogy to explain or, to be more precise to explain away, large-scale political violence. In such instances, government spokesmen, social control agents and the mass media tend to resort to a corrupter–corrupted model. The dichotomy between normal and sick people is replaced by a bifurcation between the wickedness of the few and the innocence of the many. The corrupted are portrayed as being largely innocuous and even irreproachable because they acted not of their own free will but under the influence of others. Their actions, like those of the sick deviant, are non-volitional and, therefore, politically irrelevant.[4]

In certain instances, the delegitimation of violent dissidents goes beyond impugning their status as political actors. They are not even granted recognition as human beings. Terrorists, for instance, are frequently referred to as beasts and barbarians, or compared to Nazis and other groups whose subhuman status is taken as a given. Even protesters are portrayed in this way. Thus, contemporary images of demonstrators are strikingly similar to Le Bon's classic description of the crowd at the turn of the century:

> By the mere fact that he forms part of an organized crowd, a man descends several rungs in the ladder of civilization. Isolated, he may be a cultivated individual; in a crowd he is a barbarian – that is, a creature acting by instinct. He possesses the spontaneity, the violence, the ferocity, and also the enthusiasm and heroism of primitive beings.[5]

The dehumanization of non-state actors who engage in violence enables the state to take extreme countermeasures against them without compromising its own humanity. Clearly, however, every kind of delegitimation provides the powers-that-be with a justification for overlooking the dissenters' political demands and placing them under the jurisdiction of one social control agency or another.

Terrorists, and others who engage in political violence, occasionally respond to these denials of their status as political actors or human beings by repudiating responsibility for their actions. They use the agentless passive form, for instance, in order to portray their violence as the work of impersonal forces rather than as the result of human choice. However, this kind of response is the exception rather than the rule. Perpetrators of political violence invariably use justifications rather than excuses; they accept responsibility for their actions but deny the pejorative quality associated with them.[6]

Moral justifications for non-state violence tend to take the form of what Sykes and Matza referred to in a somewhat different context as an appeal to higher loyalties.[7] It is illegal but legitimate.[8] Breaking the law, dissidents insist, is permissible and even admirable because it is in the service of a more important norm. Fighting for the nation and against the infidel are the best documented examples of this phenomenon. However, they are by no means the only ones. Ideologies of every description have provided the justification for contravening the law of the land and engaging in violence.

The moral arguments in favour of the resort to violence are often reinforced by a pragmatic one. Dissidents contend that it is impossible to accomplish their goal, or even to get their message across to the government and/or the public at large by peaceful means. Experience has taught them that engaging in violence is the only way to achieve their aims. It is the strategy of last resort.

But terrorists and other perpetrators of non-state violence devote more time and energy to unfavourable depictions of the enemy than they do to favourable portrayals of themselves. Using the contrast principle diverts attention from their own actions and, more importantly, blames them on the state. The powers-that-be are criticized for both their actions and inaction. They are accused of sins of commission and omission alike.

Allegations concerning state inaction find their clearest expression in justifications for crime control vigilantism.[9] Government failure to ensure the security and wellbeing of its citizens is regarded as a breach of the social contract. They are therefore no longer bound by its restrictions and can, indeed must, take the law into their own hands in order to fill the vacuum. In certain cases this general argument is backed up by references to specific national lore such as the American vigilante tradition or the Zionist belief in self-reliance. Norms that originated on the frontier are extended inland and applied to the country as a whole.

Vigilantism is by no means limited to crime control. It is directed against those who make the laws as well as those who break them. Thus, regime-control vigilantism aims at changing the establishment in order to make the superstructure into a more effective guardian of the base. Convinced of the fact that those in power have deviated from the true path, this particular brand of vigilante tries to force them into changing course. Although the target of violence is different, the rationale is the same. Once again, vigilantism is justified in terms of the government's failure to live up to expectations.[10]

The allegations concerning crimes of commission are made in a wide variety of provocation stories. Some focus on specific actions of the government against the perpetrators of violence themselves or those who they claim to represent. Others relate to the structural violence of the system as a whole. The message, however, is always the same. The dissenters' resort to violence is simply a response to that of the enemy. It is balanced, or even outweighed, by previous actions of the powers-that-be. It was they who set the process in motion.

This counter-denunciation, or what Maurice Tugwell has aptly referred to as guilt transfer,[11] finds its clearest expression in the war of labels between the dissidents and the government. Rather than simply depicting the state and/or its agents in negative terms, those who engage in violence refer to them in exactly the same way as they themselves are labelled – as terrorists, criminals and even subhumans. By portraying the enemy in general, and/or the direct victims of violence in particular in these ways, dissidents try to justify their behaviour both in their own eyes and the eyes of others. The pigs, whoever they may be, are simply getting what they deserve.

This recharacterization of the enemy is the clearest indication of the way in which the legitimacy of violent non-state actors is inextricably interwoven with that of the state. Their deeds, they insist, are a justified response to the prior actions or inaction of the enemy. Whilst accepting responsibility for their behaviour, non-state actors place the blame elsewhere. Self-legitimation is based, to a large extent at least, on the delegitimation of the powers-that-be.

THE STATE AND VIOLENCE

The proclivity to study stigma contests about non-state actors is due, in part at least, to the influence of Weber's definition of the state. Paradoxically, however, the large body of research that has accumulated draws attention to its major weakness. Not only do non-state actors claim legitimation for their violent actions, they also try to delegitimize those of the state. The exclusive right of the government can never be taken as a given. It always has to be fought for on the political battlefield.

Criticism of the state use of force is, of course, not limited to those non-state actors who actually resort to violence. Government policy can, and often does, lead to much broader stigma contests. Significantly, however, the issues remain essentially the same. These controversies are also concerned with the state use of force, and its failure to prevent non-state actors from doing so. They too revolve around the actions and inaction of the powers-that-be.

States, in common with non-state actors, often develop a binary code that distinguishes between a series of sacred and profane elements. By identifying themselves and their country with the former components and the enemy with the latter ones, those in power justify wars and other kinds of state violence.[12] Internal opponents may, of course, reject the code entirely. More frequently, however, they just disagree with the way in which it is applied. Engaging in a process of reclassification, they remove the differences between the warring sides. The protagonists are either as good or as bad as each other. There is, therefore, no justification for the state's resort to violence.[13]

Governments invariably engage in semantics in order to fend off criticism of their actions. The terms violence and force are used with reference to the legitimate and illegitimate imposing of one's will on another respectively. Consequently, those in power invariably refer to non-state actors as resorting to violence, and to themselves as using force. As David Riches has pointed out:

> 'Violence' is very much a word of those who witness, or are victims of certain acts, rather than of those who perform them ... When a victim invokes the notion of violence they make a judgement not just that the action concerned causes physical hurt but also that it is illegitimate ... 'Physical hurt done to others' counts as violence only in social contexts. In a negative sense, the salient context in this respect is the state. The physical force employed by the state is government ('political organization') and not violence.[14]

In a similar vein, many scholars have made a distinction between two kinds of terror – agitational and enforcement[15] or insurgent and repressive[16] – and attributed them to non-state actors and states respectively. The latter, they insist, also resort to terror. However, those holding the reins of power restrict the use of the terms to the inducement of fear by non-state actors. If and when governments engage in such behaviour, they do so under a different name.

This semantic politics of violence constitutes just one part of a much broader discourse of official denial regarding the state use of force. Governments argue that nothing happened (literal denial), what really happened is something else (interpretive denial), and what happened is justified (implicatory denial).[17] Sometimes these strategies are used in sequence – if the first one fails the next one is tried and so on. More frequently, however, they appear simultaneously. There are, of course, contradictions between the different forms of denial but together they form a deep structure. There is an ideological rather than a logical relationship between them.

When they do engage in implicatory denial, states use similar accounts to those employed by non-state actors. Thus, governments also claim to be resorting to violence out of righteousness (appeal to higher loyalties) and/or necessity (strategy of last resort). In addition, they often engage in advantageous comparison with government critics at home and abroad and, most importantly, with those who are harmed. This argument can be either situational or historical. However, whether it is based on immediate provocations or long-standing injustices the point is essentially the same. The victims are getting what they deserve.[18]

According to Richard Leeman, the similarity between the accounts of states and non-state actors is due to the fact that those holding the reins of power commonly adopt a reflective strategy.[19] They copy the arguments of terrorists and others who resort to political violence. In actual fact, the process can and often does work in the opposite direction. Non-state actors duplicate the claims of the state. Be that as it may, the end result is the same. The verbal strategies of the different protagonists mirror each other in both form and content

Clearly, those holding the reins of power, no less than those trying to wrest it from them, have to justify their resort to violence. The legitimacy of the state use of force has to be fought for on the political battlefield. But this is by no means the only struggle that governments may be involved in. Claiming an exclusive right to the legitimate use of force bestows the concomitant duty to prevent non-state actors from resorting to violence. Consequently, the government's failure to do so may lead to an additional stigma contest. It can, and often is, attacked for not enforcing law and order.

This argument is, of course, the starting point of the vigilante ideology described in the previous section. However, it does not necessarily lead to a justification of taking the law into one's own hands. Government critics can simply demand more determined action on the part of the different law enforcement agencies. They are entreated to adopt a more resolute stance, and to ensure the safety of the country's citizens. The state must keep its side of the social contract and ensure law and order.

A series of Israeli case studies indicate that this argument is sometimes taken a step further.[20] The government is not only held responsible for failing to prevent non-state actors from resorting to violence; it is also accused of causing them to do so in the first place. Using the slippery slope argument, or what Edwin Schur somewhat cryptically referred to as the doctrine of horrible consequences,[21] opposition groups argue that the words, deeds or ideology of those in power inevitably lead to the violence of their more extreme supporters. Even if the government had not intended this to happen, it is to blame. The powers-that-be are also responsible for the unforeseen consequences of their actions.

Those in power try to rebut these allegations by offering alternative explanations for the violence of non-state actors. In each case they reject responsibility for the situation and place the blame elsewhere: on the perpetrators themselves, extreme groups, the society as a whole and perhaps most importantly, on the opposition itself.[22] In the latter case the government portrays the violence as a reaction against its critics rather than as an extension of its actions and/or ideology. Paradoxically perhaps, causal responsibility is to be found at the other end of the political spectrum.[23]

Both the claims and counter-claims focus on the alleged consequences of government policies and/or the ideology on which they are based. However, the pragmatic tone is somewhat misleading. The competing explanations are based on the rhetoric of rectitude as well as the rhetoric of rationality.[24] The outcome of a particular stance is not only an important claim in itself: it is also regarded as a criterion for judging the rightness of a cause. Protagonists of all persuasions are of the opinion that policies and ideologies can, indeed should, be judged by their consequences. Thus, although they differ regarding the etiology of dissident violence, government and opposition are agreed on a more basic point: that the violence of non-state actors constitutes valid grounds for delegitimating those who failed to prevent or even caused it in the first place.

TALES OF VIOLENCE

The previous sections have drawn attention to the way in which non-state actors and states alike use the contrast principle to legitimate their resort to violence. Invariably, those concerned draw invidious comparisons between their own behaviour and that of the current enemy. Several studies have drawn attention to the fact that those involved in nationalist struggles also make analogies between the contemporary protagonists and famous and infamous figures of yesteryear. They cite past deeds and misdeeds as justifications for conduct in the present.

The analogies made by nationalist movements take the form of narratives about earlier examples of oppression and resistance. Telling these stories involves a process of mediation by means of which past events act as a filter though which present ones are understood. Thus, Aretxaga's conclusions regarding the Irish Republican Army (IRA) are applicable to other national movements. In all of them 'individual experience is embedded in collective memory as a frame of interpretation ... history makes meaningful the present as it unfolds in existential experience, directing action in the world'.[25]

Clearly, the resort to history is not only meant to help recall the past but also to reactualize it[26] by justifying and thereby encouraging the use of violence in the present. It takes the form of a series of projective narratives that are simultaneously descriptive and prescriptive.

> They not only tell a story of the past but also map out future actions that can imbue the time of individual lives with collective values ... dictate biographies and autobiographies to come ... tell individuals how they would ideally have to live and die in order to contribute properly to their collectivity and its future.[27]

These projective narratives are therefore backed up by a martyrology of people who personified them. The life histories of those who fell in the struggle for independence are constructed in such a way that they can be portrayed as the epitome of the national ideal. Their regulative biographies[28] invariably include references to how they first learnt, then lived and finally became part of the movement's projective narrative.[29]

The collective memory goes beyond the recollection of particular historical events. Present and past examples of oppression and resistance to it are invariably incorporated into a broader metahistorical narrative. They are all understood as examples of an underlying pattern of events in the annals of the nation in question, or for that matter of nations in general.[30] Those struggling for independence are therefore acting in accordance with the laws of history, and attempting to dictate its course at one and the same time.

The form and content of state narratives is essentially similar to those of national movements fighting for statehood. They also use historical precedents to legitimate their resort to violence. In some cases, analogies are even made to pre-state examples of oppression and resistance. Those who helped to bring the nation into being act as role models for its present leaders. Their past violence is cited as a justification for the contemporary conduct of the state and those at its helm.[31]

The narratives of nationalist movements fighting for independence and states that have achieved it not only relate to the past, they also predict what will happen in the future. With good on their side, the dissidents argue, they will eventually emerge victorious. Although the battle has been and may still be a long and bitter one, success is assured. Despite the seemingly insurmountable odds, victory is inevitable. Contrary to common wisdom right is might, and it will therefore ultimately prevail.[32] State narratives also tell of a longstanding struggle between the forces of good and evil, and promise that the former will eventually be victorious. However, the content of these stories is very different or, to be more precise, diametrically opposed to that of the dissidents. There is a total inversion of roles and a completely different forecast of the final outcome of the conflict. The dissidents deserve to, and therefore will be, defeated. It is only a matter of time until the resistance is crushed and order restored.

Tales of violence of state and non-state actors alike provide a classic example of Bruner and Gorfain's contention that 'any given telling takes account of previous and anticipated tellings, and responds to alternative and challenging stories'.[33] In fact, not only do the narratives of both sides mirror each other; in certain cases the protagonists even appropriate the history of their opponents in order to show that they are, in fact, the real victims of the violence. The inversion of roles is accompanied by an attempt to usurp the suffering of the other side.[34]

This is not to suggest, of course, that there is a unanimity of views within a particular nation concerning the resort to violence. The past is also a contested terrain on the internal front. Those opposed to the use of force by non-state actors or the state itself make analogies to other historical events or interpret the same ones differently. In certain instances this either leads to, or arises from, the adoption of an alternative metahistorical narrative. Those concerned see not just a particular event but the past as a whole in a totally different light.[35]

Whilst all these mnemonic battles relate to the question of what actually happened in the past, this is never the focus of concern. Protagonists of all persuasions are less interested in the issue of historical truth than they are in learning the lessons of history. Both the proponents and opponents of violence are able to cite earlier instances of oppression and resistance in support of their stance. History is flexible enough to be used by all.

PROEM

From the foregoing review of the literature it is clear that 'the pattern of violence and its civil legitimacy is more complicated than the state-centered paradigm suggests'.[36] Governments can and often do get involved in a wide variety of stigma contests. Some focus on the use of violence by the state, others revolve around its failure to prevent the violence of others. In certain instances the controversies are restricted to the perpetrators themselves; on other occasions they involve a much broader range of protagonists. Critics, both internal and external, condemn the government for its sins of commission and omission alike.

Previous studies have concentrated on one or other of these stigma contests and therefore failed to fully grasp the complexity of the situation. The present research tries to overcome this drawback by analyzing the different controversies together. It opens with an examination of the verbal strategy of non-state actors who engage in violence (Chapter 2) and then moves on to the broader debates about the state's use of force (Chapter 3) and its failure to prevent non-state actors from doing so (Chapters 4 and 5). This is followed by a discussion of the way in which protagonists of all persuasions turn to history as a source of justification for their violent actions (Chapter 6). It shows how they each use the past to legitimate their present behaviour and to delegitimate that of their ideological opponents.

All but one of the controversies took place in a single society (Israel) during the same period of time (1977–84).[37] It is therefore possible to examine both the similarities and the interaction between them. In particular, the study that follows analyzes the convergence between the different stigma contests and the way in which they merge together into a widespread concern about the violent nature of Israeli society and a broad debate about the legitimacy of those at its helm. The process is similar to that found in moral panics about the threat to law and order. In this case, however, it focuses on those at the centre rather than on the periphery of the body politic.

In the concluding chapter the focus of attention moves from rhetorical interpretation to sociological analysis. Berger and Luckmann's concept of symbolic universes[38] is used to help understand the reasons why controversies concerning the state as the perpetrator of violence in its own right, and as the auxiliary to the violence of others, are particularly common in Israeli society. This contextualization of the debates leads, in turn, to a consideration of the theoretical implications of the research findings. The book concludes with an analysis of the way in which they both necessitate, and make possible, the refinement of current ideas about the boundary-maintenance functions of deviance.

Before embarking on these tasks though, it is imperative to undertake a more basic one. Our study must begin with an examination of the Israeli body politic in general, and during the period under investigation in particular. A basic knowledge of its major protagonists and the changing relationships between them is a necessary prerequisite for understanding everything that follows.

NOTES

1. H.H. Gerth and C. Wright Mills, *From Max Weber: Essays in Sociology* (New York: Oxford University Press, 1969), p. 78. Italics in original.
2. Both images figure prominently in the official and public reaction to urban riots. Time and again, they are attributed to the criminal riff-raff or to wild youngsters who are intent on exploiting the ghetto situation rather than trying to improve it. See for instance, Joe R. Feagin and Harlan Hohn, *Ghetto Revolts: The Politics of Violence in American Cities* (New York: Macmillan, 1973), pp. 6–12.
3. Stephen Schafer, *The Political Criminal: The Problem of Morality and Crime* (New York: Free Press, 1974), p. 139.
4. Jock Young, 'Mass Media, Drugs and Deviance', in Paul Rock and Mary McIntosh (eds), *Deviance and Social Control* (London: Tavistock Publications, 1974), pp. 247–51.
5. Gustave Le Bon, *The Crowd: A Study of the Popular Mind* (London: T. Fisher Unwin, 1960), pp. 32–3. Le Bon went on to argue that crowds can be heroic as well as criminal. 'It is they rather than isolated individuals that may be induced to run the risk of death to secure the triumph of a creed or an idea ... All depends on the nature of the suggestion to which the crowd is exposed.'
6. Marvin B. Scott and Stanford M. Lyman, 'Accounts', *American Sociological Review* 33/1 (February 1968), p. 47. Dissenters even use acclaiming tactics to maximize responsibility for their violent behaviour and/or its desirability. For further details see Barry R. Schlenker, *Impression Management: The Self-Concept, Social Identity and Interpersonal Relations* (Monterey, CA: Brooks/Cole, 1980), pp. 162–4.
7. Gresham M. Sykes and David Matza, 'Techniques of Neutralization: A Theory of Delinquency', *American Sociological Review* 22/6 (December 1957), p. 669.
8. The conflict between legality and legitimacy finds its clearest expression in the courtroom. Sometimes, dissidents take the opportunity to turn their trial into a political one and to explain why their resort to violence was justified, even though it was against the law. On other occasions they take the argument a step further by insisting that the state has no right to judge them and refusing to take part in the trial.
9. See H. Jon Rosenbaum and Peter C. Sederberg, 'Vigilantism: An Analysis of Establishment Violence', *Comparative Politics* 6/4 (July 1974), pp. 548–51.
10. Ibid., pp. 556–9.
11. Maurice A.J. Tugwell, 'Guilt Transfer', in David C. Rapoport and Yonah Alexander (eds), *The Morality of Terrorism: Religious and Secular Justifications* (New York: Pergamon Press, 1982), pp. 275–89.
12. Philip Smith, 'Codes and Conflict: Toward a Theory of War as Ritual', *Theory and Society* 20/1 (February 1991), pp. 114–21.
13. Ibid., p. 123.
14. David Riches, 'The Phenomenon of Violence', in David Riches (ed.), *The Anthropology of Violence* (Oxford: Basil Blackwell, 1986), p. 3.
15. Thomas Perry Thornton, 'Terror as a Weapon of Political Agitation', in Harry Eckstein (ed.), *Internal War: Problems and Approaches* (New York: Free Press of Glencoe, 1964), p. 72.
16. Alex P. Schmid and Jenny de Graaf, *Violence as Communication: Insurgent Terrorism and the Western News Media* (London: Sage Publications, 1982), p. 59.
17. Stanley Cohen, *States of Denial: Knowing About Atrocities and Suffering* (Cambridge: Polity, 2001), pp. 101–86. Cohen also draws attention to the fact that governments sometimes partially acknowledge that they are at fault for their use of force, and describes the different way in which they do so.
18. Ibid., pp. 109–12.
19. Richard W. Leeman, *The Rhetoric of Terrorism and Counterterrorism* (New York: Greenwood Press, 1991), pp. 71–89. Leeman is highly critical of the strategy and has proposed the adoption of a non-reflective one.
20. The case studies and an ideal-type model are included in Gerald Cromer, *The Writing was on the Wall: Constructing Political Deviance in Israel* (Ramat Gan: Bar Ilan University Press, 1998).
21. Edwin M. Schur, *The Politics of Deviance: Stigma Contests and the Uses of Power* (Englewood

Cliffs, NJ: Prentice Hall, 1980), pp. 144–5.
22. Ibid., pp. 141–8.
23. This argument is strikingly similar to the perversity thesis according to which the attempt to push society in a certain direction will result in it moving in the opposite one. For further details see Albert O. Hirschman, *The Rhetoric of Reaction: Perversity, Futility and Jeopardy* (Cambridge, MA: Harvard University Press, 1991), pp. 11–12.
24. Joel Best, 'Rhetoric in Claims Making: Constructing the Missing Children Problem', *Social Problems* 24/2 (April 1987), pp. 116–17.
25. Begona Aretxaga, 'Striking With Hunger: Cultural Meanings of Political Violence in Northern Ireland', in Kay Warren (ed.), *The Violence Within: Cultural and Political Opposition in Divided Nations* (Boulder, CO: Westview Press, 1993), pp. 244–5. Aretxaga drew attention to the tendency to overlook these cultural factors in etiological studies of terrorism because of the emphasis on political causalism. On this point see also Khachig Tololyan, 'Cultural Narrative and the Motivation of the Terrorist', *Journal of Strategic Studies* 10/4 (December 1987), pp. 217–20.
26. This term is borrowed from Yosef Hayim Yerushalmi, *Zakhor: Jewish History, Jewish Memory* (Seattle, WA: University of Washington Press, 1982), pp. 44–5.
27. Tololyan, 'Cultural Narrative', p. 218.
28. Ibid., p. 230.
29. Gerald Cromer, *Narratives of Violence* (Aldershot: Ashgate, 2001), pp. 24–9.
30. Ibid., pp. 20–4, 37–8.
31. See for instance Myron J. Aronoff, 'Establishing Authority: The Memorialization of Jabotinsky and the Burial of Bar Kochba's Bones in Israel under the Likud', in Myron J. Aronoff (ed.), *The Frailty of Authority* (New Brunswick, NJ: Transaction Books, 1986), pp. 120–2.
32. Cromer, *Narratives of Violence*, pp. 20–4.
33. Edward M. Bruner and Phyllis Gorfain, 'Dialogic Narration and the Paradoxes of Massada', in Edward M. Bruner (ed.), *Text, Play and Story: The Construction and Reconstruction of Self and Society* (Washington, DC: American Ethnological Society, 1984), p. 60.
34. See for instance Coresh Barnur, 'Rhetoric in the Cycle of Terror: The Coverage of the Coastal Road Incident and the Litani Operation in the Israeli and Palestinian Press' (unpublished MA thesis, Bar Ilan University, Ramat Gan, 1998; in Hebrew), pp. 81–8.
35. Studies of both Christian and Jewish groups have drawn attention to the conflict between religious and secular readings of national history. See for instance Khachig Tololyan, 'Martyrdom as Legitimacy: Terrorism, Religion and Symbolic Appropriation in the American Diaspora', in Paul Wilkinson and Alasdair M. Stewart (eds), *Contemporary Research in Terrorism* (Aberdeen: Aberdeen University Press, 1987); and Hilda Schatzberger, *Resistance and Tradition in Mandatory Palestine* (Ramat Gan: Bar Ilan University Press, 1985; in Hebrew), pp. 70–111.
36. Philip Smith, 'Civil Society and Violence: Narrative Forms and the Regulation of Social Conflict', in Jennifer Turpin and Lester R. Kurtz (eds), *The Web of Violence: From Interpersonal to Global* (Urbana, IL: University of Illinois Press, 1997), p. 111.
37. The controversy concerning racism that is analyzed in Chapter 5 took place immediately after the period of Likud rule. However, it is included in this book because the dispute revolved, to a large extent at least, around the question of whether Menachem Begin and his colleagues were causally responsible for Meir Kahane's election to the Knesset and subsequent rise in popularity.
38. Peter L. Berger and Thomas Luckmann, *The Social Construction of Reality: A Treatise in the Sociology of Knowledge* (Garden City, NY: Doubleday, 1966), pp. 92–128.

2

The Body Politic

SUI GENERIS

Israel has always been characterized by a bewildering number and an extremely high turnover of political parties.[1] Not only does the Knesset (Israeli parliament) include representatives of many lists at any one time; the constant splintering, renaming and recombining of parties leads to a situation where at each election, certain lists enter the Knesset for the first, and maybe the last time. From this vantage point, at least, Israeli politics seems a very fickle affair.

Dividing the myriad parties into three rival camps – labour, revisionist and religious – leads to a very different view of the situation.[2] In contrast to the constant flux of parties, this tripartite division constitutes a permanent feature of Israeli political life. Not only does each camp represent one of 'the major visions that animated first those who dreamed up a Jewish State, and then those who shaped the dream into the reality of present-day Israel';[3] despite the dramatic increase in the size of the electorate and highly significant changes in its composition, they have received roughly the same proportion of votes in each election. In this respect, at least, Israeli politics has been characterized by a remarkable stability.

However, this is also not the whole story. Long before the Likud assumed the reins of power in 1977, important changes were taking place, both within and between the camps. The 'upheaval', as it widely came to be known, was not a sudden transformation, it was rather the culmination of a number of long-term developments within the Israeli body politic. These changes can be analyzed in terms of both the parties involved and the ideologies they represent. A brief look at these two perspectives will hopefully provide some idea of the context in which the different stigma contests took place.

THE END OF DOMINANCE

Maurice Duverger argued that a party can achieve dominance even though it never has, and, 'short of a miracle', never will win a parliamentary majority. It merely has to be numerically larger than the other parties for a considerable period of time. The party's influence, Duverger insists, is more important than its strength:

> A party is dominant when it is identified with an epoch; when its doctrine, ideas, methods, its style so to speak, coincide with those of the epoch ... A dominant party is that which public opinion *believes* to be dominant. Even the enemies of the dominant party, even citizens who refuse to give it their vote, acknowledge its superior status and its influence; they deplore it but admit it.[4]

But, as Duverger was at pains to point out, this situation is bound to come to an end sooner or later.

> Domination takes the zest from political life, simultaneously bringing stability. The dominant party wears itself out in office, it loses its vigour, its arteries harden ... Every domination bears within itself the seeds of its own destruction.[5]

Although written with the European and Anglo-American experience in mind, Duverger's analysis is highly relevant to the Israeli situation. It helps understand both the lengthy dominance, and the subsequent decline of Mapai.[6]

Mapai and, after its merger with other parliamentary factions, Labour or the Alignment,[7] received the largest proportion of votes in eight successive elections. Although it never won an outright majority and was therefore forced to set up coalition governments, Mapai always retained the premiership and controlled the major ministries. Its representatives always held the key portfolios in both domestic and foreign affairs.

Mapai's dominance was by no means limited to brute political power. It was also of a spiritual nature. Throughout the period of the Yishuv (the pre-state Jewish settlement in Palestine), the party was identified with the pioneering values of socialist Zionism – the dominant ideological trend of the Jewish national movement. In 1948 it was presented with an opportunity shared by few parties in democratic politics – that of presiding over the creation of a state. David Ben-Gurion and other party leaders were, from that time on, renowned as the founding fathers of the modern state of Israel.

Mapai's conquest of the political centre enabled it to determine which parties were on the periphery: 'It had the authority to define the boundaries between the permissible and the unacceptable.'[8] This was particularly important when it came to setting up a coalition. On each occasion, the party leader chose a different set of partners according to the exigencies of the moment. Ben-Gurion, however, who was Prime Minister for more than a decade, always made a point of excluding two parties from his calculations, working to the principle: 'no Herut or Maki'. According to his view, the right-wing Herut movement led by Menachem Begin was on a par with Maki, the Israeli Communist Party. Both were beyond the pale.

With the passage of time, marked changes have taken place in the fortunes of Mapai and Herut. This is partly due to demographic factors. Those sectors of the population who registered support for Herut – Jews of Oriental origin and younger voters – were steadily increasing, thereby accounting for a larger share of the electorate, while groups traditionally supportive of Labour were shrinking in size. However, this is by no means the whole story. Important developments also took place within Herut itself, and in Israeli politics in general.

Although Herut was usually the party that received the second largest proportion of votes in the Knesset, it perceived itself and was perceived by others as a party in permanent opposition rather than as the leading force in an alternative coalition, or a partner in the existing one. Slowly but surely, however, Menachem Begin adopted a number of courses of action, each of which was designed to move Herut towards the centre of the political spectrum. The most important of these strategies was the development of a series of alliances with more moderate parties in the civil camp. This led to the creation of a parliamentary bloc (Gahal) with the Liberals in 1965, and of the more broadly based Likud immediately after the Yom Kippur War. While political scientists differ as to whether this strategy of concentration entailed a moderation of traditional Herut politics or just a change in the movement's image, they are all agreed that it constituted one of the major reasons for Herut's growing legitimacy.

This trend received its strongest impetus from the inclusion of the newly created Gahal bloc in the National Unity government that was set up on the eve of the Six Day War. Menachem Begin's willingness to override the opposition of party hardliners and join hands with his long-standing rivals, provided a clear indication of his determination to move toward the centre of the political spectrum. And, no less importantly, Prime Minister Levi Eshkol's decision to invite Gahal in the first place showed how much it had already achieved in this respect. Agreeing to share power with Herut, albeit in a situation of national emergency, signified that the party had finally shed its pariah status. By the time Gahal resigned from the government in 1970 over US Secretary of State William Rogers' peace plan, it had become a viable alternative to the Alignment.

The Yom Kippur War was also particularly important in this regard. The surprise attacks in Sinai and on the Golan Heights led to a severe crisis of authority which was immediately felt at the ballot box. In the elections that took place just six weeks after the cease-fire agreement, the Alignment managed to hold on to power, but lost one-fifth of its seats in the Knesset. This dramatic decline prompted the party to revamp its leadership. In particular, Yitzhak Rabin, Chief of Staff in the Six Day War, was chosen to replace Golda Meir as Prime Minister. However, this and other changes were to no avail. The government was seriously weakened by high inflation, widespread labour unrest and, above all, by a series of corruption scandals. Rabin himself was forced to resign after a news reporter revealed that his wife had an undeclared bank account in the United States. His arch-rival, Shimon Peres, assumed the premiership, only to lead the Alignment to its first defeat at the polls just one month later. In May 1977 the Likud assumed the reins of power and Menachem Begin became the sixth Prime Minister of the State of Israel.

Israeli politics entered a completely new era. After the upheaval 'the dominant party structure gave way to the polarized situation of two large blocs competing for supremacy'.[9] Paradoxically, however, this momentous change was not due to a marked increase in support for the Likud. The immediate causes of the upheaval lay elsewhere.

The most important factor was the meteoric rise of the newly formed Democratic Movement for Change (DMC), led by Yigal Yadin, the second Chief of Staff of the Defence Forces and a world-renowned archaeologist. It garnered 11.6 per cent of the vote and, as a result, won 15 seats in the Knesset. According to many political analysts, the DMC provided a viable option for a large number of people who were highly disillusioned with the ruling party but nevertheless found themselves unable to vote for the traditional opposition one. It enabled them to express their discontent without actually going over to the other side.

The second development occurred within the religious camp. The two major parties – the National Religious Party (NRP) and the ultra-orthodox Agudat Yisrael both underwent important changes. The NRP broke its historic partnership with Labour Zionism, and Agudat Yisrael abandoned its traditional neutral stance in order to join the Likud-led administration. In doing so they radically changed the political map in Israel. Henceforth, the religious and civil camps joined forces in the ongoing struggles about the borders of the State of Israel and the nature of the society within them.

THE RETURN OF IDEOLOGY

Scholars of many disciplines have drawn attention to the ideological bent of party politics during the pre-state Yishuv. This was, of course, the 'natural heritage' of groups founded in Eastern Europe at the turn of the century – 'a time and a place where political dialogue was invested with the tone and temper of religious warfare'. However, local factors also played a crucial role in this regard:

> [T]he political situation in Israel was similar to that which prevailed in Eastern Europe. In both, ideologies were developed by groups that had no share in the responsibility for government. In such an atmosphere, political organizations are encouraged to distinguish themselves from one another by eschatological vision rather than actual performance.[10]

In addition,

> the institutional arrangements of the World Zionist Organization, the early battleground of the parties, was hospitable to schismatic politics, since elections were based on proportional representation, in which even the smaller factions could hope to hold the balance of power. Hence the usual incentive to broaden a movement's ideological base was attenuated.[11]

The 'government-in-exile mentality' continued after the establishment of the state, and the system of proportional representation was transferred to the Knesset. Nevertheless, there was a distinct waning of ideological fervour after independence was attained. In common with other new societies, the nascent Jewish state began to evolve from an ideological democracy to a territorial one, in which 'the important ties and vital interests of the vast majority of its citizens stem from non-ideological considerations, derived from the sheer fact of living in the country'.[12]

Almost 20 years after independence this trend came to an abrupt end. In the wake of the Six Day War there was a 'renewed ideologization' of Israeli politics (Galnoor, 1980: 128). The question of the boundaries of the state was no longer just a theoretical one, and it therefore returned to the top of the national agenda. Not surprisingly, the renewed debate about the future of the occupied or liberated territories[13] mirrored, to a large extent at least, the controversy that raged between Labour and Revisionist Zionism during the period of the Yishuv.

David Ben-Gurion and other leaders of the 'state-in-the-making' accepted the recommendations of the Peel Commission. They favoured the principle of partition because it endorsed the idea of Jewish sovereignty, albeit not over the whole of Palestine. The Revisionists, however, completely rejected the report. Not only were they opposed to giving up part of western Palestine; they advocated Jewish sovereignty over the entire Land of Israel on both sides of the River Jordan. Indeed this remained part of the Herut party platform until 1965, and Menachem Begin and his colleagues refused to accept the 1948 armistice border with Jordan right up until the Six Day War two years later.

After the war, the Alignment concentrated its efforts on establishing a number of settlements along the Jordan Valley in order to provide Israel with 'defensible borders'. With the passage of time, internal divisions within the party and external pressures from more right-wing groups led to the establishment of settlements elsewhere on the West Bank. However, the overall aim of the government was still to ensure continued Israeli control over those areas deemed crucial for national security whilst leaving open the possibility of returning other parts of the occupied territories in exchange for peace.

The situation changed entirely when the Likud assumed the reins of power. Its settlement policy was specifically designated to preclude the possibility of the West Bank being returned to Jordan or becoming part of a Palestinian state. At first, the government relied on the ideologically motivated members of the Gush Emunim settler movement to populate the heartland of Judea and Samaria. Determined to 'create facts on the ground' the Likud-led administration soon turned its attention to areas close to Jerusalem and Tel Aviv and appealed to people's pockets rather than their principles. The government offered financial inducements such as cheaper housing, high mortgages and handsome tax subsidies to those who were prepared to move to the other side of the Green Line. During the seven years of Likud rule the number of settlements increased by 450 per cent and the number of settlers by twice that amount. According to many observers, the situation had reached the point of no return.

In signing the peace treaty with Egypt, the Likud-led administration agreed to return the entire Sinai Peninsula and to work towards Palestinian autonomy on the West Bank and the Gaza Strip. Many of Menachem Begin's most faithful supporters saw this as a betrayal of the Land of Israel and began to work through new political parties, extra-parliamentary groups and even a terrorist underground to prevent the implementation of the Camp David Accords. However, most political analysts saw things very differently from the radical right. They were of the opinion that Menachem Begin regarded both aspects of the treaty as a way of ensuring Israel's continued control of the West Bank. Ceding the Sinai Peninsula to Egypt and autonomy to the Palestinians was the logical conclusion of the government's settlement policy rather than in total contradiction to it.

A similar situation existed with regard to the War for the Peace of the Galilee. It was presented as an operation designed to oust the Palestine Liberation Organization (PLO) from Southern Lebanon and thereby prevent its attack on Israel's northern settlements. In actual fact, however, it aimed to destroy the entire PLO infrastructure up to and including Beirut. Liquidating the organization would allow the Likud-led administration to negotiate with the local Palestinian leaders that it had assiduously nurtured. This, in turn, would enable Menachem Begin to implement his autonomy plan and retain Israeli control, if not sovereignty, over the West Bank.

Whereas the hawkish policy of the Likud was a direct continuation of old Revisionist beliefs, the maximalist stance of the National Religious Party (NRP) was markedly different from its pre-Six Day War attitude. Until then the party focused its attention on religious issues. In accordance with what Zalman Abramov aptly referred to as the doctrine of coercion,[14] it exploited its parliamentary strength to further the twin goals of withdrawal from, and conquest of Israeli secular society. However, under the influence of the Young Guard faction and the Gush Emunim settler movement, the NRP began to relate to a much broader range of issues. This transition from the politicization of religion to the religiosization of politics[15] was most marked in the realm of foreign affairs. Guided by what they felt to be the only true interpretation of traditional texts and contemporary Jewish history, the political and spiritual leaders of the NRP became staunch advocates of a Greater Israel. The Jewish people, they argued, have a divine right to the entire land. Consequently, the 'territories for peace' formula is not just a grave threat to national security, it is also a blatant disregard of God's will.

For the religious right the attainment of independence, the subsequent ingathering of the exiles and especially the 'miraculous victory' in the Six Day War were all indicative of the fact that we are living in an era of redemption.[16] This is not to suggest, however, that religious Zionists adopted a passive stance towards the unfolding of history. In fact, exactly the opposite was the case. They saw themselves as God's partners in the process of redemption and the eventual establishment of the messianic kingdom. This belief found its clearest expression in the prominent role played by the knitted skullcap generation in both the legal and illegal settlement of the territories. The religious right was the vanguard of the holy crusade for the Land of Israel. 'No other force competed with it in supplying spiritual vitality and depth ... It was the main ideological bolster of the hawkish position.'[17]

Despite the growing influence of the religious right, the National Religious Party experienced a marked decline in popularity. It suffered a 50 per cent drop in support in the 1981 elections. Having emphasized the importance of the territorial issue, almost to the exclusion of all others, the NRP saw many of its staunchest and long-standing supporters shift their allegiance to Techiya, a new movement that was set up with the explicit purpose of preventing the implementations of the Camp David Accords, and the Likud that had signed them. Although disillusioned with Menachem Begin's policies, many religious advocates of a Greater Israel wanted to ensure that the Likud remained the largest party and therefore be asked to form the next government. The Alignment would only be worse.

A MULTI-CLEAVAGE SOCIETY

The future of the territories was by no means the only area of disagreement between the rival camps. It was part of a much broader struggle over the nature and significance of the Jewish state. While these controversies had always been on the national agenda they became much more intense during the period of Likud rule. The years 1977–84 witnessed wide-ranging debates about the Jewish dimensions of Israeli society. They related to traditional and civil religion alike.

As has already been pointed out, the ultra-orthodox Agudat Yisrael abandoned its traditional neutral stance after the upheaval. Although still refusing to join the government it assumed the chairmanship of the powerful Knesset finance committee in exchange for signing a formal agreement to support the new Likud administration. In addition, the government gave its support to a series of legislative measures that were designed to protect the ultra-orthodox community from the influence of Israeli secular society and to enforce its norms on it.[18] These laws, together with the steep rise in financial allocations to Agudat Yisrael and other ultra-orthodox institutions caused a great deal of animosity amongst certain sectors of the secular population. They complained that their standard of living was declining, and their lifestyle being cramped as a result of the new political alliance.

The socialist and statist civil religions associated with Labour Zionism were plagued by a widespread legitimation crisis long before the 1977 upheaval. The declining influence of the once dominant camp was due, to a large extent at least, to long-term developments within Israeli society. It was clearly intensified, however, by two external conflicts. Both the euphoria that followed in the wake of the Six Day War and the shock caused by the Yom Kippur War just six years later led to a decline in the influence of the two secular belief systems and their capacity to legitimate the Jewish state. Consequently they ceded pride of place to the 'new civil religion' that was much more sympathetic towards the Jewish tradition in general and its religious aspects in particular.

These developments had an important effect on the Labour camp. It gradually moderated its earlier hostile attitude, and adopted an increasingly conciliatory stance towards Jewish tradition. Nevertheless, the new civil religion was more closely associated with Revisionist and religious Zionism. Its growing ascendancy was both a major cause and an important result of the Likud's rise to power and its subsequent alliance with the National Religious Party. They agreed not only about the borders of the Jewish state but also on the raison d'être for them. Both parties based their territorial claims on the historic rights of the Jewish people. The religious and secular right alike relied on the divine promise concerning 'the land of our forefathers'.[19]

These differences with regard to both traditional and civil religion were compounded by the intensification of long-standing ethnic divisions in Israeli society. Although ethnic parties ran in every Knesset election they met with little success. They did not gain a seat after 1951 and usually disappeared from the political scene by the next elections. This was due, to a large extent at least, to the widespread tendency to delegitimate such lists. Despite the proliferation of parties, ethnicity was generally considered to be an inappropriate basis for political activity. It was regarded as being inconsistent with the widely accepted ideal of the melting pot and the ingathering of exiles.

Another reason for the failure of the ethnic lists was the long-standing tendency of Jews of Eastern (North African or Asian) origin to vote for Herut, and subsequently for Gahal and the Likud, the larger parliamentary blocs in which it was incorporated. Many reasons have been offered for this particular voting preference. However, they fall into three broad categories: a widespread feeling of having been economically and culturally discriminated against by the ruling Labour Party; an underlying similarity between the traditional authoritarian culture of the Oriental immigrants and the paternalistic style of Menachem Begin; and the firm belief in the need for a hawkish foreign policy. The Arabs, they argued, only understand the language of force.[20]

Both these ethnic patterns were clearly evident during the period of Likud rule. In 1981, Tami, a new Sephardi (mainly Moroccan) party won three seats in the Knesset, the best showing of an ethnic list since the first national elections. Even more importantly, the struggle between the two major parties was marked by 'an unprecedented crystallization of ethnic differences'. Two-thirds of Likud supporters were of Sephardi origin, and as many as 70 per cent of those who voted for the Alignment were of Ashkenazi/Western background. The first and second Israel were pitted against each other more than ever before.

These observations provide a classic example of Horowitz and Lissak's observation concerning Israel as a multi-cleavage society. They contend that the overlap among them intensifies conflict because 'instead of distinct cleavages each with a single dimension, there is one dominant cleavage with numerous dimensions, each of which exacerbates the others'.[21] This was particularly the case during the period of Likud rule. The conflict over the future of the territories was compounded by disagreements on other ideological issues and the growing rift between the different ethnic groups within Israeli society.

Political scientists have argued that this multifaceted polarization led to a marked increase in intrasocietal violence during the period of Likud rule.[22] While this is undoubtedly a correct and important reading of the situation, the present study adopts a very different perspective. It focuses on how the stigma contests about this and other forms of political violence intensified the polarization between the different camps rather than on the extent to which they were one of its unfortunate consequences. Emphasis is placed on the way in which violence or, to be more precise, the debates that it generated, led to a deepening of the divisions within Israeli society, and a serious questioning of the policies and ideologies of those at its helm.

NOTES

1. As many as 27 parties ran for the 16th Knesset in January 2003. Thirteen of them received 1.5 per cent of the vote, which is the minimum necessary to gain a seat in the Israeli Parliament.
2. Daniel J. Elazar, 'Israel's Compound Polity', in Ernest Krausz (ed.), *Politics and Society in Israel* (New Brunswick, NJ: Transaction Books, 1985), pp. 52–3.
3. Real Jean Isaac, *Party and Politics in Israel: Three Visions of a Jewish State* (Baltimore, MD: John Hopkins University Press, 1981), p. 2.
4. Maurice Duverger, *Political Parties: Their Organization and Activity in the Modern State* (London: Methuen, 1964), pp. 308–9. Italics in original.
5. Ibid., p. 312.
6. For two detailed applications of Duverger's analysis to the Israeli situation see Alan Arian and Samuel H. Barnes, 'The Dominant Party System: A Neglected Model of Democratic Stability', *Journal of Politics* 36/3 (August 1974), pp. 592–614; and Ariel Levitte and Sidney Tarrow, 'The Legitimation of Excluded Parties in Dominant Party Systems', *Comparative Politics* 15/3 (April 1983), pp. 295–327.
7. At the beginning of 1968 Mapai merged with Achdut Ha'avoda and Rafi to form a new parliamentary bloc – the Alignment. This union lasted until 1984, when Mapam decided to break ranks rather than participate in the National Unity Government together with the Likud.
8. Arian and Barnes, 'Dominant Party System', p. 597.
9. Dan Horowitz and Moshe Lissak, *Trouble in Utopia: The Overburdened Polity of Israel* (Albany, NY: State University of New York Press, 1989), p. 172.
10. Leonard J. Fein, *Politics in Israel* (Boston, MA: Little Brown & Co., 1967), p. 70.
11. Ibid.
12. Daniel J. Elazar and Shmuel Sandler, 'The Two-Bloc System: A New Development in Israeli Politics', in Daniel J. Elazar and Shmuel Sandler (eds), *Israel's Odd Couple: The 1984 Elections and the National Unity Government* (Detroit, MI: Wayne University Press, 1990), p. 15.
13. The way in which the territories are described by the different groups is, of course, indicative of their political stance toward them. In a similar vein, those in favour of territorial compromise refer to the areas captured from Jordan as the West Bank, and advocates of a Greater Israel insist on calling them by their biblical names – Judea and Samaria.
14. Zalman S. Abramov, *Perpetual Dilemma: Jewish Religion in the Jewish State* (Rutherford, NJ: Fairleigh Dickenson University Press, 1976), pp. 167–73.
15. Horowitz and Lissak, *Trouble in Utopia*, p. 58.
16. Negative events such as the Yom Kippur War were interpreted in a similar vein. According to the religious right, whatever appears to contradict the redemption process is, in fact, a

divine reprimand designated to cajole the Jewish people into mending its ways and, in turn, to hasten the coming of the Messiah.
17. Shlomo Deshen, 'Doves, Hawks and Anthropology: The Israeli Debate on Middle Eastern Settlement Proposals', in Gisli Pallson (ed.), *Beyond Boundaries: Understanding Translation and Anthropological Discourse* (Oxford: Berg, 1993), p. 61.
18. These measures included the introduction of a more liberal policy of exemptions from military service for religious girls, the cessation of El Al flights on the Sabbath and Jewish holidays, and severe restrictions on both abortions and autopsies.
19. Another major characteristic of the new civil religion was the belief that anti-Semitism is an endemic phenomenon rather than a response to the abnormal existence of the Jewish people in exile. However, this conviction was shared by all three camps and it may therefore have led to an easing of the divisions within Israeli society. For further details on this point see Charles S. Liebman and Eliezer Don-Yehiya, *Civil Religion in Israel: Traditional Judaism and Political Culture in the Jewish State* (Berkeley, CA: University of California Press, 1983), pp. 123–53.
20. These explanations are well summarized in Michal Shamir and Asher Arian, 'The Ethnic Vote in Israel's 1981 Elections', in Asher Arian (ed.), *The Elections in Israel 1981* (Tel Aviv: Ramot, 1983), pp. 100–3.
21. Horowitz and Lissak, *Trouble in Utopia*, p. 33.
22. See for instance Sam N. Lehman-Wilzig, *Stiff-Necked People, Bottle-Necked System: The Evolution and Roots of Israeli Public Protest 1949–1986* (Bloomington, IN: Indiana University Press, 1990), pp. 40–3; and Ehud Sprinzak, *Political Violence in Israel* (Jerusalem: Jerusalem Institute for Israel Studies, 1995; in Hebrew), pp. 75–91.

3

Terrorism

ARABS AND JEWS

President Sadat's historic visit to Israel in November 1977 was vehemently condemned throughout the Arab world. Other Arab states and the PLO objected to his apparent willingness to sign a separate peace agreement with Israel. They accused the leader of the largest and most powerful Arab nation of having given up the struggle for an independent Palestinian state. He had become a traitor to the cause.

The Sadat initiative led the PLO to abandon its traditional policy of non-intervention in the internal affairs of Arab states and its neutral stance in the disagreements between them. Yasser Arafat and President Assad issued a joint communiqué calling on the Egyptian army to resist Sadat's treason to the Arab nation, and set up the Steadfastness and Confrontation Front together with other radical Arab regimes. In addition to their diplomatic activity, the PLO turned to violence in an attempt to derail the nascent peace process. On 11 March 1978 the seaborne Deir Yassin force[1] landed on the Mediterranean coast south of Haifa. They commandeered two buses on the main coastal highway and engaged in a shoot-out with the Israeli army and police on the outskirts of Tel Aviv. The operation left 32 dead and 82 injured. It also led to an extensive curfew over the central sector of the country as the security forces searched for any members of the force who may have escaped during the hostilities.

Previous terrorist incidents invariably led to a retaliatory response of one kind or another. On this particular occasion, however, the Israeli reaction was much more extreme than usual. Three days after the attack the Israeli Defence Forces (IDF) began the Litani Operation. An army of 25,000 troops invaded South Lebanon in an attempt to destroy the PLO presence there. Three months later the Israeli army withdrew and was replaced by the United Nations Interim Force in Lebanon (UNIFIL). By then 700 people had been killed, thousands injured and scores of Lebanese villages destroyed.

Meanwhile the peace process moved forward and eventually culminated in the Camp David Accords. Egypt agreed to recognize and normalize relations with the State of Israel in exchange for a total withdrawal from the Sinai Peninsula and the granting of autonomy to the Palestinians on the West Bank and in the Gaza Strip. While the peace treaty was widely regarded as a historic breakthrough, it was vehemently opposed by the advocates of a Greater Israel. They doubted President Sadat's promises and rejected Menachem Begin's concessions in order to achieve it.

Under the rubric of the Movement to Halt the Retreat in Sinai, the leaders of Gush Emunim organized demonstrations and engaged in civil disobedience in an attempt to prevent the implementation of the agreement. A number of settlers were convinced that the withdrawal constituted a reversal of the redemption process. They regarded it as a divine signal that a major offence had been committed by the nation. There was only one sin that matched the magnitude of the setback: the continued presence of the Muslim Dome of the Rock on the Temple Mount. The conclusion was simple. They had to 'remove the abomination'. Doing so would terminate the peace process and restart the messianic one. After two years of intense theological discussion and practical planning the operation was ready. However, it was not carried out because one essential ingredient was missing. Those involved failed to gain rabbinical approval for their scheme, and it was therefore shelved.

During this time the Jewish Underground, as it widely became known,[2] also turned its attention to a more immediate problem – the personal security of the settlers on the West Bank and particularly in the ancient city of Hebron. The killing of six yeshiva (talmudic academy) students in May 1980 and of another one three years later led to two deadly responses – the blowing up of five West Bank mayors who were all prominent leaders of the Palestine National Guidance Committee, and a raid on the local Islamic college. However, it was not until April 1984 that the Underground was exposed. Thirty settlers were arrested on suspicion of having placed bombs on five Arab buses around the country.[3] While the ideas of the Underground millenarian were never translated into practice, its vigilante ideology led to increasingly indiscriminate violence against the local Arab population.

The PLO and the Jewish Underground alike tried to legitimate their resort to violence. In doing so, not only did they engage in self-defence; they also took the offensive. While the PLO attacked the various actions and policies of the Likud-led administration the Jewish Underground emphasized the inaction of Menachem Begin and his colleagues. Both groups reproached the Israeli government but they concentrated their attention on the sins of commission and omission respectively.

SINS OF COMMISSION

The PLO tried to justify the use of violence on both moral and pragmatic grounds. Organization spokesmen referred to the righteousness of the Palestinian cause and argued that there was no other way of furthering it. Armed struggle is not only a legitimate course of action, it is the strategy of last resort.

The raid on the coastal highway was meant to achieve two goals – a short-term one of the release of Palestinian prisoners being held in Israeli prisons, and the long-term one of national liberation. The Palestinians, it was argued, have the same elementary rights that people throughout the world enjoy or are deemed entitled to enjoy: 'the right to return to one's country of origin, self-determination and statehood'. These ends justify or, to be more precise, sanctify the violent means used to achieve them.

Many Palestinians had died as a result of 'their intense yearnings for the motherland and the deep sorrow created by broken promises'. This led them to the realization that the only way to achieve liberation was to engage in an armed struggle against the Jewish state. Doing so had, of course, led to heavy losses, but the suffering was of a different nature. Palestinians no longer die waiting for others to help. Rather they are killed on the battlefield, having sacrificed themselves on the altar of the motherland.

Looking at their progress so far, the PLO pointed to successes on both the propaganda and the military fronts. The organization had managed to put the Palestinian issue on the world agenda and to inflict painful losses on the Jewish state. Each operation had made the organization stronger and more resolute, but the latest one was of particular significance. The Deir Yassin force showed that 'the PLO can reach anywhere'. In doing so, it disproved 'the theory of defensible borders' and shattered 'the myth of Israeli invulnerability'.

Those who fell in the raid on the coastal highway and against the Israeli forces in Lebanon were portrayed as the apogee of the Palestinian armed struggle. They were described in the most laudatory terms, and invariably referred to as *shahidim*, martyrs who died in a holy war. The operation was immediately referred to as legendary and compared to Karameh where the PLO inflicted heavy losses on the Israeli forces that tried to destroy their command headquarters.[4] Coming as it did just nine months after the stunning defeat in the Six Day War, the bravery and courage of the Palestinians helped restore Arab dignity. Then and now, they showed that it was possible to fight with honour.[5]

The PLO was often at pains to point out that the ratio of forces – 'three tanks to one stone' – gave a very misleading impression of the situation. In purely military terms the organization was, of course, no match for the Israeli military machine. However, once other aspects of the confrontation are taken into account the Israeli advantage is seen to be a spurious one. The most important of these factors is the fierce determination of the PLO rank and file. Their staunch belief and firm resolve prompted the leaders of the organization to turn to their Arab counterparts and implore them not to be frightened of the enemy. The Israeli soldiers, they insisted, are in a state of fear and on the verge of breakdown in the face of the brave *fedayeen* and the 'iron will of the revolution'.

This determination was not regarded as an inherent characteristic of those concerned. Rather it was attributed to the worthiness of their struggle and the righteousness of their cause. The need to liberate the motherland brings out the best in people. Consequently,

> A small and determined military force can resist and even defeat a huge and arrogant army. Highly developed weaponry is not the determining factor in a war. The major component is the fighter who uses the arms to further his just cause. There is still a long and bitter struggle ahead, but in the end the revolution will be victorious.[6]

Contrary to conventional wisdom, right is might and will, therefore, eventually prevail.

The process was often conceived of in more personal terms but the end result was always the same. Organization spokesmen attributed the bravery of contemporary fighters to a desire to glorify past heroes by their own heroic deeds. Thus the *shahidim* who carried out the raid on the coastal highway were trying to follow in the footsteps of Kmal Adwan, a PLO leader who had been assassinated five years earlier in Beirut. Having sacrificed their lives they immediately became 'an eternal sign' of the struggle for the Palestinian homeland. Dalal Al-Moughrabi in particular, was held up as an example for others. Relating to the question 'why did she fight?' the obituarist in the PLO monthly, *Palestine Perspectives*, wrote:

> She crossed over to face the Israelis who occupied her home and to make a statement that Palestinians would rather die on their land in dignity than be forgotten in exile ... Dalal Al-Moughrabi finally returned to her homeland Palestine and told the world that Palestine lives. Her only choice was to make this statement by sacrificing her life. If she is to have a legacy, it is in working to build a future where Palestinians may leave behind the bitterness of exile to live in equality and peace in Palestine.[7]

By becoming a role model for her fellow countrymen and women 'Dalal's journey would begin, not end, with death.' She and others may be killed, but the revolution will continue until victory.

In common with other terrorist movements, the PLO devoted more attention to negative portrayals of the Zionist enemy than they did to these positive depictions of themselves. The highly favourable references to their own heroes were outnumbered by fierce attacks on the Jewish state. In propaganda as in battle, attack is the best form of defence.

PLO spokesmen made two conflicting claims regarding the raid on the coastal highway. On several occasions, they insisted that the Deir Yassin force had no intention of killing civilians, and that it only did so in response to the actions of the Israeli security forces. In other instances, organization spokesmen engaged in what Sykes and Matza referred to, in a somewhat different context, as denial of the victim.[8] Those killed and injured deserved their fate because

> Israel was established on the basis of confiscation of Arab land. Consequently, every Zionist is a colonialist and land-robber. All the laws of liberation movements therefore apply, and it is obligatory to drive them out.[9]

However, the contradiction between the two claims must not be allowed to hide their essential similarity. Both transferred the blame for the loss of Israeli lives from the PLO to the Jewish state.

With the beginning of the Litani Operation, the PLO turned its attention to the plight of Palestinian victims. Time and again, organization spokesmen referred to the number of people killed, injured or forced to leave their homes as a result of the Israeli invasion of Lebanon. In doing so, they often singled out the number of women and children involved so as to emphasize the inhumanity of the Israeli Defence Forces (IDF) and those at their helm. In order to drive the message home, the PLO augmented these statistics with personal accounts and dramatic photographs. The victims were not just numbers. Each one had a story and a face.

This rhetoric of victimization was invariably accompanied by a frontal attack on both the ends of the war and the means used to achieve them. Thus the PLO criticized the widespread use of cluster bombs against the Lebanese civilian population, and the resort to phosphorus bombs as part of the Israeli scorched-earth policy. More importantly, organization spokesmen repeatedly rejected the Israeli claim that the operation was carried out in response to the PLO raid on the Haifa–Tel Aviv highway a few days earlier. That attack was simply a convenient pretext for an action that the Israeli government had intended to carry out for a long time. The scale and complexity of the operation showed that it was, in fact, just another example of Israeli expansionism. Whether motivated by the long-standing desire of Zionist leaders to control the water of the Litani or a more general aspiration to extend the borders of the Jewish state, the end result was the same – yet another annexation of Arab lands and the expulsion of the local Palestinian population.

This reading of the situation led the PLO to engage in a war of labels. 'Why', they asked,

> is Palestinian violence called terrorism but Israeli violence is referred to as retaliation, reprisal or a mop-up of infestation? By what moral or legal standards can the institutionalized and organized terror perpetrated by the State of Israel on Palestinians and Lebanese be justified? Don't Israeli practices in the West Bank and Gaza constitute a form of terrorism when they include the confiscation of property, the demolition of homes, administrative detention, population expulsion and many other human rights violations?[10]

The question was, of course, rhetorical. PLO spokesmen also provided the answer:

The law is in favour of those who have tanks and planes. They can kill and destroy as they please ... The law is against those who fight for their motherland and their struggle is regarded as terrorism. Where is the law and where is justice?[11]

The PLO adopted a completely different view of the situation. Organization spokesmen were at pains to point out that they were acting in accordance with the 1948 Geneva Convention and subsequent United Nations resolutions.[12] Those fighting against the Israeli forces in Lebanon were invariably referred to as guerillas or resistance fighters. Israelis in contrast were branded as criminal, terrorist and even subhuman. Its animal-like behaviour indicated that it was indeed 'an American Zionist baby monster'.

This war of labels was accompanied by a much less common kind of inversionary discourse.[13] The PLO appropriated a number of central Jewish myths to propagate the Palestinian cause. Thus, it did not simply refer to the seemingly insurmountable odds that the organization was facing. The PLO placed the contemporary situation in the context of the biblical story of David and Goliath. The roles, however, had been reversed. With the biggest army in the Middle East, the Jews were no longer the underdogs – the Palestinians had taken their place.

The PLO complained about the extent to which the Israeli leaders used the Holocaust to mobilize support for the Zionist cause both at home and abroad. However, this did not prevent the organization from appropriating this particular episode in Jewish history.[14] It repeatedly castigated Israeli leaders for engaging in Nazi oppression and adopting SS tactics. In certain instances the PLO took this analogy a step further. They viewed the entire history of the State of Israel through the lens of the Holocaust.

> The destruction of its [Palestinian society's] fabric in 1948 was for Palestinians a holocaust (*Al Nakba*). It resulted in the political extermination of an entire nation, as manifested in land alienation, colonial settlement, demographic change, population expulsion and a reign of terror for those who remained behind. But if the 1948 *Al Nakba* involved the eviction of indigenous Palestinians by Israeli settlers, the 1967 war ushered in a pattern of organized genocide against the Palestinian people. The recent invasion of Lebanon is part of an ongoing process of systematic annihilation ... Today more than ever Zionism seems bent on administering the final solution to the Palestinian cause.[15]

The PLO also appropriated the founding myth of the Jewish people, the exodus from Egypt. Thus, an English language information bulletin, included 'A Song for a Palestinian Passover' that was based on three popular medleys from the traditional Seder service.

I

If they had taken our land and not gloated in busloads
It would have sufficed.
If they had taken our land and not said it was God's will
It would have sufficed.
If they had divided our homes among them and not said
    that we did not exist
It would have sufficed.
If they had dropped napalm and not repeated shalom
It would have sufficed.
But they did all these things.
How many the cruelties they have bestowed upon us.

II

Who knows One?
I know One: one lost homeland.
Who knows Two?
I know Two: two hands to hold a rifle.
Who knows Three?
I know Three: three tanks against one stone.
Who knows Four?
I know Four: four cities lost to us.
Four lost cities.
Three tanks coming.
Two hands only.
One lost homeland.

III

Then came the planes
That came from America
That dropped napalm
That burned our children
That once had lived
In our land Palestine.

> Then came the young men
> That once were boys
> Then came the young women
> That once were girls
> Then came the young people
> That once were children
> That now are fighters
> That fight for their land of Palestine.[16]

Gradually, the song moves from a total preoccupation with the victimization of the Palestinian people to an emphasis on its fighting spirit. Ironically, the PLO turned to Jewish history for a model of the transition from passive to active suffering and the achievement of national independence.

SINS OF OMISSION

In an essay published immediately after the exposure of the Jewish Underground, Yehuda Etzion, one of its leaders, drew attention to what he felt was a distinguishing feature of the Jewish people. As 'a kingdom of priests and a holy nation' they are not meant to simply survive. Their eternal existence derives from the unique role they are ordained to play in the divine scheme of things. The chosen people are obliged to live not only a life of existence but also a life of destiny.[17] Unfortunately, however, the Israeli government has not succeeded on either front, having failed desperately with regard to both the physical and spiritual wellbeing of the Jewish state.

The members of the Underground were full of praise for the local army commanders who were responsible for the settlers' day-to-day security. They were keenly aware of the need to take military action, both preventive and retributive, against the PLO and its supporters, and were perfectly willing to do so. However, 'their hands were tied' by the political echelons, even though the Likud-led administration was ostensibly in favour of strengthening and expanding the Jewish presence in the territories. Time and again during the course of their police interrogation and subsequent trial, the members of the Underground lambasted the government for its hesitancy and inaction. The harshest criticism was directed against Ezer Weizmann, the Minister of Defence. 'Like a man under the influence of a peace drug' he had simply become blind to reality and, therefore, made no attempt to deal with it.

Faced with a steadily worsening security situation, the members of the Underground decided to act. The government had failed to ensure the security of the settlers and they therefore had no option but to take the law into their own hands. Thus Shaul Nir resorted to the traditional vigilante argument in an attempt to justify his involvement in the Underground and a number of solo actions against Palestinians in Hebron. 'The situation is unbearable', he contended:

> Jews are unable to live in peace. They find themselves in a permanent state of insecurity. Unfortunately, the State of Israel has abandoned the claim to full sovereignty and the enforcement of law and order. This has created a vacuum that the Arab community has exploited to the full ... Under these conditions the government does not have a moral right to demand that its Jewish citizens forfeit their security in the name of a law that is not applied ... Our actions were designed to instill an awareness in the Arab population that continuing acts of terrorism and identification with them will lead to unpleasant consequences. Above all, however, they were meant to goad the Israeli authorities into enforcing law and order and to stop standing idly by when Jewish blood is spilt.[18]

The members of the Underground often backed this argument with relevant quotes from traditional Jewish sources. In particular they referred to the biblical commandment not to stand idly by the blood of your neighbour and the rabbinical injunction to kill someone first if he comes to kill you. However, the essence of the vigilante argument was perhaps best captured in an oft-quoted saying from the Ethics of the Fathers (2:6): 'In the place where there are no men, try to be one.'[19]

The particularistic aspect of this claim was by no means limited to an appeal to traditional Judaism. Members of the Underground also justified their actions by comparing them to those of Jewish heroes from the time of the Macabbees until the struggle against the British mandate in Palestine. Most importantly, they were at pains to point out that the whole raison d'être of secular Zionism had been to establish a safe haven for the Jewish people, a homeland in which they would be free from hatred and persecution. Consequently, the Likud-led administration was not only guilty of breaking the social contract that is incumbent on all governments, it was also at fault for neglecting the specific role assigned to those at the head of the Jewish state.

The traditional vigilante argument was often accompanied by an additional and seemingly contradictory claim. Time and again, members of the Underground contended that the government was not opposed to and even favoured their resort to violence. They suggested that it turned a blind eye and even gave covert support to their vigilante actions. This 'division of labour' between the settlers and the authorities enabled the latter simultaneously to carry out its policies in the territories and circumvent US criticism of them. The Underground strengthened rather than weakened the government's hand in its dealings with enemies and allies alike.[20]

Those members of the Underground who engaged in vigilante actions tried to use both arguments during the course of their trial. They contended both that their resort to violence was a response to government inaction and that it was supported by the Likud-led administration. However, both claims were disallowed. The judges dismissed them as irrelevant. Some of the defendants subsequently fired their lawyers and rested their case. The government's policy regarding Arab terror was the very heart of the Underground's stance. Once this line of argument was rejected the defendants simply had no leg to stand on.[21]

Those involved in the plan to blow up the Dome of the Rock offered a much wider variety of accounts. They too, however, emphasized the inaction of successive Israeli governments and the consequent need to fill the void. In fact, the millenarian terrorists' criticism of the powers-that-be was much more comprehensive. Not only had the country's leaders failed to safeguard the physical existence of its citizens; they had also completely overlooked their spiritual destiny.

The advocates of millenarian terrorism were particularly critical of Israeli policy regarding the Temple Mount. Since the Six Day War, successive governments had allowed Judaism's most holy place to remain under the control of the Muslim religious authorities – the Waqf – and thereby be desecrated. In doing so, the country's leaders had brought the divine redemption process to a halt. It would only be renewed after the destruction of the Dome of the Rock and the return of the Temple Mount to Jewish hands. The task was incumbent on the government of Israel. However, since it had failed to do so, there was no option but to step into the breach. Once again, 'in a place where there is no man, try to be one'.

Yehuda Etzion referred to both these themes – the inaction of the government and the consequent need for individuals to fill the void –

in a booklet on the Temple Mount that he wrote and published while serving his prison sentence.

> [King] David's acquisition of the Temple Mount was an eternal one in the name of all Israel. It has never expired and will never do so ... It is the one we are now called upon to effect ... The arm of the people in this matter is, of course, the State of Israel ... but the general feeling is that the Mount is a holy place for the Muslims and that they own it ... This terrible situation in which the Muslim claim to ownership of the Temple Mount is supported by the State of Israel prompted a number of people to consider and plan an operation that would expose the simple truth that the People of Israel have exclusive sovereignty over the Temple Mount, and remove the Waqf from our most holy place ... We demand that the court recognize the fact that it is the failure of the state to do this that constitutes the background for our 'crime' ... Ever since our soldiers conquered the Mount 17 years ago, all the authorities have consistently avoided taking any action, like an ostrich that buries its head in the sand. How long can we remain silent and do nothing?[22]

Etzion and his colleagues were particularly critical of the leaders of the national religious camp in this regard. Even though they believe that the State of Israel is 'the dawn of our redemption' they had failed to take the requisite action to speed up the messianic process. It is not enough to turn to God and ask for His intervention. 'Prayers have to be transformed into deeds.'

> We cannot sit and wait for the Holy One Blessed Be He to perform miracles and do all the work for us ... Our soldiers entered the Temple Mount to conquer it, and we must complete the conquest by removing the forbidden alien presence ... The purification of the Temple Mount will prepare people's hearts for understanding and advancing our total redemption.[23]

The similarity between the millenarian argument and the vigilante one is clear. They both related to the failure of the country's leaders to do what was incumbent on them, and the consequent need for individuals to fill the void. However, the two accounts also differed in one important respect. While the vigilante argument focused on the failure of the Likud-led administration to deal with current physical threats, the millenarian one concentrated on its lack of concern about the country's spiritual future. They related to the government's lack of will and lack of vision respectively.

SINNER OR SINNED AGAINST?

The accounts of the Jewish Underground and the PLO were aimed at essentially different audiences. While the settlers focused their attention on their fellow citizens on both sides of the Green Line, the Palestinians tried to influence public opinion in the 'reactionary Arab states' and the Western world. Both groups, however, tried to justify their resort to violence by arguing that it was in reaction to the prior sins of the Israeli government. Of course, the Likud-led administration viewed things very differently.

The Israeli government attacked the members of the Underground for taking the law into their own hands. Comparisons between their actions and those of Menachem Begin, Yitzhak Shamir and other Likud leaders against the British during the mandatory period were dismissed out of hand. While Etzel (Irgun Zva Leumi/National Military Organization) and Lehi (Lohamei Herut Yisrael/Fighters for the Freedom of Israel) led to the establishment of the State of Israel, the Jewish Underground was causing it serious harm. The vigilante actions had already hindered rather than helped the settlement efforts on the West Bank, and had the plans to blow up the Dome of the Rock been carried out it might have set off a regional and even a world war. The Underground was courting disaster.

The National Religious Party, which was a key member of the Likud-led administration, made essentially the same arguments with regard to vigilante terrorism, although they were sometimes couched in traditional Jewish terms rather than being based on secular notions of a social contract. Criticism of the plan to blow up the Dome of the Rock focused on the roles of human and divine action in the messianic process. Party leaders, political and spiritual alike, attacked Yehuda Etzion's theology of active redemption as a clear deviation from the major tenets of religious Zionism. The Underground was 'forcing the end', and therefore guilty of false messianism.

Despite these harsh criticisms, the Jewish Underground was greeted with a certain amount of ambivalence by some government ministers and other leaders of the Israeli right.[24] This was clearly not the case with regard to the PLO. It was always referred to in the most damning terms and often compared to the Nazis. Palestinian claims regarding the attack on the coastal highway were completely rejected. Menachem Begin and his colleagues insisted that the Deir Yassin force had intended to kill as many Israelis as possible from the outset, and that those who were murdered did not deserve their fate. Both these counter-arguments found their clearest expression in the Prime Minister's statement to the Knesset two days after the attack:

> The entire nation mourns the men, women and children who were killed just because they were Jews. All those murdered were law-abiding and honest people who never caused harm to anyone ... From the moment they landed on the shore, they killed Jews simply because they are Jews. They murdered a young woman, took over a taxi and killed its passengers, commandeered one bus and then another, and fired in every direction in order to kill the Jews just because they are Jews.[25]

The PLO claims concerning the Litani operation were also rejected out of hand. Time and again, government spokesmen argued that the civilian casualties were unavoidable. There is no such thing as a sterile war, and in this case it was particularly unlikely because the PLO placed its fighters inside Lebanese villages. It purposely increased the likelihood of civilian casualties and then blamed them on the Israeli security forces.

The Israeli government did not only relate to the consequences of the Litani operation, it also tried to explain why it had invaded Lebanon in the first place. At a press conference soon after the operation began, Menachem Begin insisted that it was not an act of revenge. Rather it derived from the inalienable right of any nation to defend itself. Subsequently, Chaim Herzog, the Israeli Ambassador to the United Nations, made a similar point but with more specific reference to the situation at hand. He also insisted that the Israeli response was not a matter of revenge, and then went on to argue that it was completely justified because:

> In the light of the PLO's declared intention to repeat atrocities like the one carried out in Israel last Saturday, the Government of Israel was left with no alternative. It acted in accordance with its legitimate national right of self-defense, the inherent right to defend its territory and population and to ensure that no more barbaric attacks will be launched against it in the future. The aim of the Israeli Defense Forces' operation was not revenge or retaliation ... It was to clear the PLO once and for all from the areas bordering on Israel, which it used mercilessly for repeated aggression against my country.[26]

Statements of this nature were accompanied by seemingly contradictory ones about the acceptability and even necessity of taking revenge. Recalling his thoughts on first hearing about the terrorist attack during a 'peace mission' to New York, Ezer Weizmann, then Minister of Defence, wrote:

> Thirty years of war and terrorist actions have created a kind of fixed 'exchange rate' for vengeance and retribution – a balance of debits and credits in the blood bank ... the compelling necessity to hit back, or feasibility of exercising restraint depend on the number of coffins on either side of the border.[27]

This line of thought was most succinctly captured in the first briefing of General Rafael Eitan, the Deputy Chief of Staff, to senior officers on the eve of the Litani Operation. Quoting the famous Hebrew poet, Chaim Nachman Bialik, he declared that, 'Satan has not yet invented revenge for a small child.'[28] Eitan's intent was clear – not to negate the soldiers' feelings of revenge but to generate them. They were to repay the PLO for its past actions as well as to prevent further ones in the future. They were to look back and forward simultaneously.

The government felt that there was no need to respond to the more far-reaching claims of the terrorists. PLO allegations regarding Israel's expansionist desires went unanswered. Clearly, however, repeated statements to the effect that Yasser Arafat was intent on the destruction of the State of Israel constituted an indirect reply. They implied that the coastal road attack was not provoked by the expansionist policies of the Likud government or, for that matter of earlier Labour ones. It was the very existence of the Jewish state that the PLO was fighting against.

MORALITY PLAYS

The Jewish Underground and the PLO criticized the Likud-led administration for its inaction and actions respectively. While the settlers attacked the government's failure to safeguard the existence and advance the destiny of the Jewish state, Palestinian spokesmen assailed its continuing and even escalating violence against their fellow-countrymen. However, this difference in emphasis must not be allowed to hide the important similarities between the two groups. Not only did they both try to legitimize their resort to violence by portraying it as a response to the prior sins of the Likud, each group appropriated Israeli values and symbols in its attempt to do so.

Both during their police interrogation and their ensuing trial, the members of the Jewish Underground insisted that it was they and not the government who had acted in accordance with traditional Zionist values such as settling the land and self-defence. In addition, they claimed to be the true exponents of religious Zionism and the teachings of its revered leader, Rav Avraham Kook. In a similar vein, the PLO portrayed the Deir Yassin force as the latest standard bearers of Palestinian heroism. In addition, however, the organization spokesmen appropriated privileged biblical texts and the primary myth of Israeli society – the Holocaust – in support of their right to an independent state and the use of violence to achieve it. Time and again, the Palestinians assumed the role of the Jews to show that they were the victims and not the victimizers in the Arab–Israeli conflict.

But the PLO rhetoric of victimization was by no means limited to the dramatization of injury.[29] It also included references to the shift from passive to active suffering, and the promise that the organization would eventually be victorious and see the return of the Palestinians to their motherland. In a similar vein, the Israeli government did not only relate to the harm inflicted by the PLO. Menachem Begin, in particular, drew attention to the way in which the Jewish people had moved from destruction to resurrection, and asserted that they would ultimately destroy the terrorists and achieve peace and tranquility in their homeland.

The parallelism and the conflict between the Palestinian and Israeli discourse could not be clearer. The stigma contest took the form of two similar but competing morality plays. Both sides portrayed themselves as the forces of light confronting the forces of darkness. These two elements of the rhetoric – casting and altercasting – were accompanied by a third one – forecasting.[30] Palestinian and Israeli leaders alike insisted that eventually good would triumph over evil and that their nation would eventually prevail.

NOTES

1. The force was named after an Arab village on the outskirts of Jerusalem, the inhabitants of which were massacred by the Etzel (Irgun Zva Leumi/National Military Organization) and Lehi (Lohamei Herut Yisrael/Fighters for the Freedom of Israel) in April 1948 during the Israeli War of Independence. PLO spokesmen often pointed out that the attacks on Deir Yassin and the bombing of the refugee camps of unarmed Palestinians during the Litani Operation were carried out by 'the same famous terrorist – Menachem Begin'.
2. Members of the Underground and their supporters placed the term Jewish Underground in

inverted commas because they felt it was inappropriate. Religious doves put inverted commas around the word Jewish to express their belief that both millenarian and vigilante terrorism were a clear violation of Jewish law. This was part of a wider debate of how the group should be referred to. A number of writers in *Hatzofe*, the official paper of the National Religious Party, emphasized the need to distinguish between 'the underground activity of individuals', amongst the Jewish settlers and 'organized Arab terror'. In contrast, B. Michael, a columnist in the independent daily *Ha'aretz*, contended that those involved should be depicted and treated in exactly the same way as Arabs who 'use savage tactics against civilians – as a band of murderers'.

3. Sentences handed down by the Jerusalem Magistrates Court, or, after appeal, by the Israel Supreme Court, ranged from four months to life imprisonment. However, as a result of the remission of sentences for good behaviour and presidential pardons for ill health and other reasons, all the members of the Underground were released within less than five years.
4. The members of the Deir Yassin force were also compared to the Muslim fighters who helped Saladin defeat the Christian crusaders at the Battle of Hittin in 1187.
5. Organization spokesmen often backed up their own laudatory remarks with statements attributed to the Israeli Minister of Defence and Chief of Staff regarding the bravery of the PLO fighters in Lebanon.
6. *Palestine Altara*, 27 March 1978.
7. *Palestine Perspectives*, May 1978.
8. See Gresham M. Sykes and David Matza, 'Techniques of Neutralization: A Theory of Delinquency', *American Sociological Review* 22/6 (December 1957), p. 668.
9. This quotation from a PLO radio broadcast is taken from Coresh Barnur, 'Rhetoric in the Cycle of Terror' (unpublished MA thesis, Bar Ilan University, Ramat Gan, 1998; in Hebrew), p. 68.
10. *Palestine Perspectives*, May 1978.
11. *Palestine Sheun*, April 1978.
12. The PLO also drew attention to the fact that it was the first national liberation movement to be accorded observer status at the United Nations.
13. See David E. Apter, 'Democracy and Emancipatory Movements: Notes for a Theory of Inversionary Discourse', *Development and Change* 23/3 (July 1992), pp. 139–73.
14. The appropriation of the Holocaust is particularly significant because of the central role that it played in the Israeli response to PLO terrorism in general and the attack on the coastal highway in particular. For further details on this point see Hillel Nossek,'The Narrative Role of the Holocaust and the State of Israel in the Coverage of Salient Terrorist Events in the Israeli Press', *Journal of Narrative and Life History* 4/1 and 2 (1994), pp. 119–34; Barnur, 'Rhetoric in the Cycle of Terror', pp. 33–40, and the discussion on pages 114–18 of this book.
15. *Palestine Perspectives*, May 1978.
16. *Palestine*, 31 May 1978. The first part of the PLO song is based on a medley that praises God for all the favours he has bestowed on the Jewish people. Each verse is followed by the refrain, 'It would have sufficed.' The second section derives from a song that lists the central features of Judaism – one God on heaven and earth, two tablets of the covenant, three patriarchs, four matriarchs, five books of Moses, and so on. The final segment is reminiscent of 'Only One Kid', the last verse of which reads as follows:

> Then came the Holy One blessed be He and destroyed the angel of death, that slew that slaughterer, that killed the ox, that drank the water, that quenched the fire, that burned the stick, that beat the dog, that bit the cat, that ate the kid, that my father bought for two zuzim. Just one kid, just one kid.

17. Yehuda Etzion, 'From the Laws of Existence to the Laws of Destiny', *Nekuda* 75 (6 July 1984).
18. Quoted in Haggai Segal, *Dear Brothers* (Jerusalem: Keter, 1987; in Hebrew), p. 159.
19. In other instances, the citing of Jewish sources took the form of what Sykes and Matza ('Techniques of Neutralization', p. 669) have aptly referred to as an appeal to higher loyalties. Thus, one member of the Underground wrote:

I also acted to protect Eretz Yisrael [the Land of Israel] from the Arab terrorists who don't want any Jews to live here. We have a mitzvah [commandment] to settle Eretz Yisrael ... If we were to allow the Arabs to continue to hurt us, it could be that a lot of Jews wouldn't come here and then we wouldn't be fulfilling the mitzvah.

See Era Rapaport, *Letters from Tel Mond Prison: An Israeli Settler Defends the Act of Terror* (New York: Free Press, 1996), p. 255.
20. Gush Emunim made a similar argument with regard to the establishment of illegal settlements in the territories.
21. The members of the Underground also protested the fact that they were standing trial while those who carried out the terrorist attacks in Hebron and elsewhere were being freed in an exchange agreement between Israel and the Popular Front for the Liberation of Palestine.
22. Yehuda Etzion, *The Temple Mount* (Jerusalem: Caspi, 1985; in Hebrew), pp. 2–5.
23. Ibid., p. 4. Etzion also related to possible international reactions to the blowing up of the Dome of the Rock. He dismissed the prophecies of doom about a regional or world war and insisted that the opposition would be limited to the 'realm of declaration'. For further details see Segal, *Dear Brothers*, pp. 117–18.
24. On this point see Gerald Cromer, *The Writing was on the Wall: Constructing Political Deviance in Israel* (Ramat Gan: Bar Ilan University Press, 1998), pp. 61–83.
25. *Divrei HaKnesset* 82 (1978), p. 2013. *Divrei HaKnesset* is the official record of the deliberations of the Israeli Parliament.
26. William V. O'Brien, *Law and Morality in Israel's War with the PLO* (New York: Routledge, 1991), p. 43.
27. Ezer Weizmann, *The Battle for Peace* (New York: Bantam Books, 1994), pp. 265–6.
28. *Ma'ariv*, 15 March 1978. The Deputy Chief of Staff made a similar point in his autobiography:

The war began after the terrible bloodbath on the coastal highway. Besides ensuring that the terrorists will not continue killing, the IDF waged a war of revenge. The order was to annihilate the terrorists.

See Rafael Eitan, *The Story of a Soldier* (Tel Aviv: Ma'ariv 1985; in Hebrew), p. 163.
29. See James A. Holstein and Gale Miller, 'Rethinking Victimization: An Interactional Approach to Victimology', *Symbolic Interaction* 13/1 (Spring 1990), p. 105.
30. This threefold division is derived from the author's analysis of the propaganda of Lehi. For further details see Gerald Cromer, *Narratives of Violence* (Aldershot: Ashgate, 2001), pp. 35–6.

4

War

THE WAR FOR THE PEACE OF GALILEE

In reprisal for a PLO attempt to topple King Hussein, Jordanian forces killed thousands of Palestinian refugees. The events of what came to be known as Black September prompted the organization to move its centre of operations to Israel's northern neighbour, to Lebanon. The long-standing weakness of the central government and the plethora of militias made it easy for the PLO to establish itself there, and the large number of refugees provided a reservoir of recruits for the organization. From 1970 onwards it quickly set up bases in southern Lebanon, took control of many refugee camps and even certain parts of the capital, Beirut. Within a short time the PLO had become 'a state within a state'.

The frequent PLO attacks on Israel's northern settlements usually met with a restricted response. However, as has already been pointed out, the action of the Deir Yassin force on the major coastal highway led to the much more extensive Litani operation. Four years later, in June 1982, the attempted killing of Shlomo Argov, the Israeli ambassador to the United Kingdom, set in motion a process of escalation that soon culminated in another invasion of Lebanon. On this occasion it was referred to as a war rather than just a campaign – as the War for the Peace of Galilee.

As evidenced by the name, the only declared aim of the war was to create a 40-kilometre PLO-free zone, in order to ensure that Israel's northernmost settlements would be out of range of the organization's artillery fire. Menachem Begin assured the country that this would be achieved within 48 hours, which was indeed the case, but the war continued unabated. The government, or at least the Defence Minister

Ariel Sharon, had other undeclared goals in mind, and they necessitated a much deeper incursion into Lebanese territory.[1] Within a matter of days Israeli troops reached the outskirts of Beirut, and they subsequently took over certain sectors of the capital.

The first stage of the invasion, the one directed at distancing the PLO from the Israeli border, received almost unanimous public support. Nearly everyone was in favour of the war. However, as the 'real' aims of the military operation became clear, and its human and other costs spiralled, the consensus began to dissipate.[2] For the first time since the establishment of the state, a war generated serious debate among politicians and public alike. As the hostilities continued, they questioned both its ends and the means used to achieve them.

A WAR OF CHOICE

Opposition leaders drew attention to the fact that Menachem Begin rarely used the traditional term, the Israeli Defence Forces. He invariably referred to them as the Israeli army. This particular nomenclature, they argued, was not just a matter of semantics. It reflected a basic difference of opinion between the rival camps regarding the functions of the military, and the circumstances in which it was permissible to take up arms against Israel's enemies.

Yitzhak Rabin, a former Chief of Staff and Labour Prime Minister, spelt out his party's policy in this regard. The role of the IDF, he declared, is limited to defending the State of Israel, its citizens and its vital interests. There is no moral right to use force or practical advantage to be gained from doing so, in pursuit of the nation's political goals.[3] Consequently, Rabin recalled elsewhere, we never worked on the premise that it is possible to force the enemy to accept peace terms that are desirable to Israel, or to achieve an overall solution to the Israeli–Arab conflict. The battlefield is not an alternative to the negotiating table.[4]

S. Yizhar, the renowned novelist made a similar point in a highly emotional dispatch from the war front. Writing in the Histadrut (General Federation of Labor) daily, *Davar*, he addressed the question as to when it was right to go to war:

> Never, or only when there is no other option whatsoever. As the very last option to deal with the most basic threat. With regard to any other

> matter however serious, it may be, and even if it can only be dealt with great difficulty – no ... With regard to all other threats and dangers war is too extensive, too weighty, too final. The crushing of a war is more destructive than the threat it was meant to eliminate. The external menace becomes an internal one to the soul of the nation and undermines its very foundations.[5]

These and other statements in favour of what is widely referred to as the policy of no-choice wars provided the basis for the critique of the invasion of Lebanon.[6] Thus, S. Yizhar went on to argue that engaging in a big, extensive and total war is not only disproportionate; it also leaves the basic issue of 3 million Palestinians unresolved. Time and again Yitzhak Rabin contended that the war was based on the mistaken assumption that it is possible to reach a political solution by military means. The invasion, once it went beyond the 40-kilometre zone, was therefore doomed to failure.

Of course, Menachem Begin and his colleagues tried to rebut these criticisms of the war. Answering a no-confidence motion in the Knesset just two days after the invasion, he insisted that Israel was simply exercising its inherent right of self-defence that is enshrined in Clause 51 of the United Nations Declaration of Human Rights. The Jewish people, the Prime Minister declared, were no longer an exception in this regard. The State of Israel has the same rights as every other nation, 'No more, and no less.'[7] Ariel Sharon made a similar point. In an article entitled 'The Nature of a Defensive War', he argued that,

> We have conducted a war of initiative against terror, the culmination of which is the campaign in Lebanon that is designed to totally eradicate it from a state that is controlled by the PLO with the support of Syria ... We were in a position where it was possible to determine that PLO terrorism would eventually bring upon us a total war in a place and time not convenient for us, and in a situation that would lead to much greater loss of life ... We therefore engaged in a war of defence, one of our most just wars.[8]

As the war continued, Menachem Begin began to adopt a different and even contradictory stance. In a commencement address to the Staff and Command School that was subsequently published in Israel's two most widely read newspapers, he accepted that the war was a war of choice. Although the PLO endangered the lives of Israeli citizens and

Jews living in the Diaspora it did not constitute a threat to the existence of the state. Nevertheless, the Prime Minister insisted, the War of the Peace of Galilee was justified.

Menachem Begin cited previous wars, both international and national, in support of the government's decision to declare war on the PLO in Lebanon. Had the French countered the German invasion of the Rhineland in March 1936, he argued, the Nazi regime would have been defeated before it had the opportunity to build up its mighty military machine and the Second World War would have been avoided.[9] Turning to the local context Begin went on to argue that the high price paid in Israel's three no-choice wars – the War of Independence, the Yom Kippur War and the War of Attrition – as compared to the relatively low number of soldiers killed and injured in the two wars of choice – the Sinai Campaign and the Six Day War – also showed the wisdom of taking the military initiative. For the Prime Minister, the lessons of history were clear.

> The conclusion, based on international relations and our own national experience, is that there is no obligation to conduct a war only when there is no other option. There is no moral commandment which says that a nation must or may fight only when its back is to the sea, or it is on the edge of the abyss. A war of this nature is likely to lead to disaster and even to a holocaust. The opposite is the case. A free, sovereign peace-loving nation which hates war and cares about security must create the conditions in which a war, if it is necessary, should not be a war of no-choice. The conditions must be such – and their creation depends on human wisdom and action – that one should emerge from war to victory with the fewest possible casualties.[10]

In his 'Reply to Menachem Begin', Shimon Peres took issue with the Prime Minister's reading of both the international and national situations. The Labour leader rejected the analogy to Nazi Germany — 'a phenomenon that has no parallel in the history of humankind' – as inappropriate, and offered a very different interpretation of the events leading up to the Sinai Campaign and the Six Day War. In both cases, Peres argued, Israel found itself in a no-choice situation. It had no option but to take up arms against its Arab neighbours.[11]

Some opposition leaders adopted a slightly different stance. They accepted Menachem Begin's contention that the Sinai Campaign was a war of choice. Without exception, however, these spokesmen were at pains to point out that, as such, it was a deviation from the traditional Israeli doctrine. In all other cases, Labour only decided to take up arms when there was no alternative. Unfortunately, the Likud had hallowed the exception rather than follow the rule.

Government critics did not only relate to the issue of *jus ad bellum*; they were also concerned with the question of *jus in bello*. Politicians and protesters alike drew attention to both the ends of the war and the means used to achieve them. Concluding his reply to the Prime Minister, Shimon Peres argued that even those in favour of engaging in a war of choice have to consider the appropriate way of doing so.

> In a war of choice is it not necessary to choose the means? Are the bombing of Beirut, the cutting off of the water supply, electricity and food indispensable? ... The massive bombardment of an Arab capital was not necessary. The IDF siege, and the very talented management of the negotiations by Philip Habib, could have led to the removal of the terrorists from Beirut and their transfer to other places ... I never believed in the theory that the end justifies the means.[12]

Opposition spokesmen were at pains to point out that Israel must maintain its traditionally high standards in this regard rather than adopt the much lower ones of its enemies. 'What is permissible to them', they argued, 'is forbidden to us.' Political and military leaders alike simultaneously complained about these double standards and that the army was, in fact meeting them. Thus, after six months of fighting the IDF spokesman claimed that,

> The Israeli soldier conducted himself with moral standards superior to those held by the fighting men of any other army under similar circumstances. The IDF paid for its care in protecting civilian lives by sacrificing the element of surprise and thereby suffered heavy casualties. However, the IDF and Israel were judged with a double standard by members of the world community who conveniently overlooked how they themselves reacted in similar wartime situations in the not too distant past.[13]

Critics at home and abroad had nothing to complain about. The Israel Defence Forces were to be commended for their purity of arms. Not only the aims of the war, but also the means used to achieve them were beyond reproach.

THE BIG PLAN

Categorizing the War for the Peace of Galilee as a war of choice raised the question of whether the decision to invade Lebanon was a wise one. This was particularly the case after the IDF achieved the only declared purpose of the war – the creation of a PLO-free zone in south Lebanon. As the hostilities extended further north, an increasing number of people argued that the war had become counterproductive. Its goals were not being achieved or were even unachievable, and it was causing a great deal of harm at both the individual and national level.[14]

As the war extended beyond the 40-kilometre zone it became increasingly clear that the invasion had a number of hidden goals. They included the expulsion of the PLO and the Syrian forces from the whole of Lebanon and the installation of a Christian-dominated government that would sign a peace treaty with Israel. Looking further afield, those responsible for the conduct of the war believed that the weakening of the PLO would pave the way for the emergence of new leaders on the West Bank who would be prepared to implement the autonomy plan agreed upon in the Camp David Accords and, in a rather roundabout fashion, to the overthrow of King Hussein. Both developments, it was hoped, would reduce the pressure for the establishment of a Palestinian state in the occupied territories.[15]

Critics of the war were at pains to point out that its single achievement was both short-lived and limited to the military realm. By the end of 1983, the PLO had returned to south Lebanon and, as a result of Israeli actions against Yasser Arafat and his followers, the organization's international standing improved in leaps and bounds. Although Israel inflicted heavy losses on the Syrian land and air forces, President Assad refused to withdraw his troops from Lebanon. The much vaunted domestic reordering failed completely. The peace treaty was never ratified by the Lebanese Parliament, and was eventually cancelled. Not surprisingly, therefore, the situation on the West Bank and in Jordan remained unchanged – both Yasser Arafat and King Hussein remained fully in control.

Opposition spokesmen contended that the failure to achieve the goals of the war was compounded by its negative consequences. First and foremost, of course, there was the loss of lives. Government critics drew attention to the mounting number of soldiers who had been killed or injured in the hostilities. Many of them also cited the human toll that the Lebanese had paid as a result of the invasion. Time and again, they expressed their regret for the thousands of innocent citizens and refugees who had lost their lives, and the widespread destruction that had occurred in the latest round of the conflict between Israel and its Arab neighbours.

Government critics drew attention to many other negative aspects that the war was having on Israeli society. Foremost amongst these were the economic and political ones. Politicians and publicists alike analyzed the different ways, direct and indirect, in which the hostilities were having a detrimental influence on the national economy. They also examined the political price that Israel was paying both at home and abroad. As the war continued, its detractors lamented the nation's increasingly pariah status in the international community and the growing dissension and polarization within the country. In both cases, the government was blamed for not having taken these negative consequences into account, or for failing to give them the salience that they deserved. The decision to take up arms is not just a military one. All possible repercussions must be taken into account before entering the fray.

Opposition spokesmen also criticized the government's lack of foresight in the military realm. They argued that those responsible for the conduct of the war did not have a clear understanding of the situation in Lebanon. Political and military leaders alike underestimated the intensity of the hatred between the warring factions and the perseverance of the Syrians and, even more so, of the PLO. As Aharon Yadlin, a former Labour Minister of Education, pointed out, Sharon, Eitan and others should have realized that 'it is impossible to break a national movement with the use of force, and it is doubtful whether a war can crush a guerilla movement or prevent acts of terror'.[16] Military superiority is not a guarantee of success on the battlefield.

This was particularly the case with regard to the invasion of Lebanon. Ariel Sharon had a 'big plan' in mind even before he became Minister of Defence, and he began to implement it immediately after taking office. The fact that all the goals of the war had to be kept secret had a crucial influence on the conduct of the war. In particular, it precluded the possibility of a frontal attack on the Syrian forces in Lebanon and thereby reduced the chances of achieving the covert aims of the campaign. Somewhat ironically perhaps, those responsible for the conduct of the war, a war of choice, were unable to choose the appropriate means to assure victory. Their options and, therefore, their chances of success, were severely limited.

Those responsible for the conduct of the war took a very different view of the situation. Political and military leaders alike not only believed that they had made the right choices regarding the goals of the invasion, they were also sure that it would be completely successful. Thus, towards the end of August, after two months of fighting, Menachem Begin confidently predicted that

> We can already look beyond the war. It will come to an end ... and there will be an extended period of peace ... because other Arab countries are not able to attack the State of Israel ... Of course, it is impossible to fix a time. It could be that the land will be quiet for 40 years, maybe less, maybe more. However, it is clear that with the end of the fighting in Lebanon we will have many years of honouring peace agreements and peaceful relations with the different Arab countries.[17]

But things turned out very differently. The fighting in Lebanon continued unabated, and peace seemed further away than ever.[18] According to Ze'ev Schiff and Ehud Ya'ari, both prominent military and Arab affairs correspondents, there was only one source of consolation: 'A misguided war', they argued, 'is a stage that every nation goes through on its way to political maturity.'[19]

SABRA AND SHATILLA

According to an official government statement, the Israeli Defence Forces entered West Beirut on 6 September 1982 in order to prevent 'the danger of violence, bloodshed and chaos'. However, their presence in the Lebanese capital did not stop the Phalangists from massacring more than 300 Palestinians in the Sabra and Shatilla refugee camps three days later. Having assumed responsibility for restoring law and order, the Israeli government came under heavy criticism both at home and abroad. Menachem Begin and Ariel Sharon in particular were lambasted for their lack of foresight in allowing the Phalangists to enter the camps. Their long record of violence against Palestinians and their determination to avenge the assassination of the President-elect Bashir Jemayael should have alerted the government to the imminent danger. As Shimon Peres pointed out in the Knesset debate on 'The Entry into West Beirut and its Grave Consequences':

Why was it necessary to endanger our soldiers and to take upon ourselves a responsibility that is not ours, a responsibility that we cannot possibly bear? ... There is no need to be a political genius or a hallowed commander; it is enough to be a village policeman to understand that the militias that were more agitated than ever because of the murder of their leader, were likely to kill even innocent people. Is this a surprise? Is this a development that we could not foresee?[20]

The leader of the opposition then turned his attention to the government's failure to respond to the unfolding of events in Sabra and Shatilla. 'If it approved the entry of the Phalangists into the camps,' he asked,

Where was the monitoring? Where was the reporting? Where was the follow-up? Who kept an eye on what was happening? ... Why did it take the television cameras to reveal what was going on? Did none of the ministers know? Did they not express an interest? Is this a children's game? Do they have eyes and not see? Do they have ears and not hear?[21]

These blunders before and during the massacre, many critics argued, were compounded by the government's subsequent reaction. They pointed to Begin's and Sharon's apparent lack of contrition, their refusal to accept responsibility for the tragedy and their tendency to blame it on everybody else but themselves. Thus, both the opposition parties and extra-parliamentary groups made frequent reference to the Prime Minister's dismissal of the worldwide criticism of Israel's role in the massacre as a blood libel, and to his subsequent jibe that 'gentiles kill gentiles and everybody blames the Jews'.[22] They also contended that official statements concerning the events in Sabra and Shatilla were replete with contradictions and half-truths. Clearly, the government had something to hide.

Notwithstanding the severity of these charges, many critics of the government were at pains to point out that the massacre was by no means a surprise. Some of them drew attention to the past record of the triumvirate or 'unholy trinity' that had been responsible for the conduct of the war. They argued that Menachem Begin's and Ariel Sharon's roles in the Deir Yassin and Kiba massacres, along with the decision of the Chief of Staff, Rafael Eitan, to reduce the sentence of soldiers found guilty of killing Palestinian civilians during the Litani campaign, were clear indications of what was in store.[23] Other critics contended that the massacre was the logical outcome of 'the unreasonable and unattainable aims of the war set by the Begin–Sharon government', or even of the more restricted War for the Peace of Galilee. Considering the violent nature of Lebanese politics, it was clear from the very beginning that Israel would eventually get embroiled in this kind of disaster.[24]

There were those who took this argument a step further. Benko Adar for instance, a columnist in the Mapam daily *Al Hamishmar*, insisted that the massacre was the result of a worldview characterized by an unrestricted belief in the use of force and a clear dichotomy between Jews and non-Jews.[25] The latter point was most forcefully made by S. Yizhar in an anthology of anti-war writings:

> Why is there this desensitization? Because in Israel today it is accepted that the world is divided into two: Jews and subhumans. Because it is accepted by many that there is Jewish blood that will not be unrequited, and the blood of subhumans. Because many claim that there is one law for Jews and another law, or no law whatsoever, for everybody else. Because out of all the concepts in the world there are just two simple ones in use – black and white. We and everybody else.[26]

Those opposed to this dehumanization of the enemy portrayed the controversy surrounding the massacre as a struggle for 'the soul of Zionism'. As in the 1981 election campaign, government critics contended that they were engaged in a battle between two cultures or moral worlds. The moral rather than the physical fate of the nation was at stake. The internal enemy, not the external one, was the real threat to the Jewish state.

The most radical critics of the war demanded that Menachem Begin and Ariel Sharon be indicted and brought to trial for failing to prevent or even aiding and abetting murder. Others viewed the massacre as a political rather than a legal issue, and argued that it should be dealt with in terms of the persons involved or the policies they adopted. While the former demanded the dismissal of the Minister of Defence or the resignation of the entire government, the latter called for an immediate withdrawal from Beirut or Lebanon as a whole. They were concerned with punishing the sins of the past and preventing further ones in the future respectively.

By far the most widespread response to the massacre was the demand for the establishment of an official committee of inquiry to investigate Israel's role in the Phalangist massacre of the Palestinian refugees. As many as 400,000 people joined a demonstration in Tel Aviv in an attempt to force the government's hand. Apolitical figures such as President Navon and even some members of the Likud administration came out in favour of the idea. They also felt that it was the only way of determining the truth about what had really happened in Sabra and Shatilla. Rejecting Menachem Begin's claim that the establishment of a committee would be understood, both at home and abroad, as an acknowledgement of guilt, his critics contended that exactly the opposite was the case. Failure to do so suggested that the government had something to hide, and that it was at least indirectly responsible for the massacre.[27]

Menachem Begin and his colleagues tried to rebut these allegations by referring to the massacre as a disaster. They did so not in order to draw attention to the enormity of the tragedy but to deny responsibility for its occurrence. What happened in Sabra and Shatilla was the result of forces beyond human control rather than the consequence of human error or evil. Israeli political and military leaders were not to blame for the tragic turn of events. Consequently, the reasons for the public outcry against the government were to be found elsewhere.

Ariel Sharon attributed the response to the massacre to the ulterior motives of those concerned. Opponents both at home and abroad had a hidden agenda. They were trying to bring down the government and force Israel to relinquish its hold on the West Bank respectively. In order to drive this message home the Minister of Defence contrasted the outrage in the wake of the Sabra and Shatilla massacre to the lack of response to similar events in other places around the world, and even in Lebanon while the Labour party was in power. Clearly, politics not principle, Sharon insisted, was the driving force behind the public outcry.

Those charged with the conduct of the war not only rejected responsibility for the massacre and explained why they had been saddled with it, they also tried to shift the blame elsewhere. Rafael Eitan, for instance, attacked Shaffik el-Wazzan, the Prime Minister of Lebanon, and Morris Draper, the United States special envoy, for having foiled Israeli attempts to make contact with the Lebanese army, thereby delaying the handing over of refugee camps to the local forces. Wherever they had managed to do so, Eitan argued, 'not a single hair on the head of a citizen had been harmed'.[28] Elsewhere, Israel successfully fulfilled the role it took upon itself on entering the Lebanese capital. Law and order prevailed.

This guilt transfer was part of a much broader attack on those who had criticized Israel's role in the massacre. Time and again, leaders of the Likud and the religious right insisted that the Jewish people had always been and were still particularly sensitive to the values and sensitivity of human life. And, as Nurith Gertz has pointed out, they always portrayed Israel as an antidote to the other nations of the world in this regard. The division of Israeli society into two cultures was rejected and replaced by a dichotomy between Jews and gentiles. Jews *qua* Jews could never display the kind of disrespect for human life that the government had been accused of. It was simply beyond the bounds of possibility.[29]

POISONERS OF WELLS

The controversy surrounding the invasion of Lebanon immediately gave rise to another source of friction. As a result of the polemic about the morality and wisdom of the military campaign, protagonists of all persuasions engaged in a fierce debate about the freedom of dissent during wartime. Thus, not only did the government defend its actions, it also questioned the right to criticize them. Opposition leaders had to go beyond attacking the war, they also had to justify their doing so.[30]

Government spokesmen contended that the lack of consensus had a negative effect on the war effort. Time and again they argued that it led to a lowering of morale in the army and to a mood of defeatism amongst the general population. For the PLO, on the other hand, the public criticism of the war was a source of encouragement, and it increased the organization's determination not to leave Beirut. The 'undermining of the government' was also thought to have a deleterious influence on Israel's image abroad. Thus, Ariel Sharon accused the opposition of 'adding fuel to the fire, the fire of anti-Semitism and blood libel', and Rafael Eitan subsequently castigated the news media and other 'professional do-gooders' for having provided Israel's enemies abroad with 'information' which they exploited to the full. 'No gentile', he argued, 'will allow himself to be more moderate than self-hating Jews.'[31]

Government spokesmen pointed to the motives of the opposition as well as to the consequences of its actions. They claimed that Shimon Peres and his colleagues were trying to further their personal or party interests at the expense of those of the nation as a whole. All they were interested in was bringing down the government and taking over the reins of power.[32] Likud leaders tried to drive this message home by pointing out that Menachem Begin had invariably given his wholehearted support to Labour governments during times of war. He had always put the interests of the nation first, and Shimon Peres should do likewise.[33]

Supporters of the war often explained, or maybe explained away, the opposition to it in psychological terms.[34] They argued, for instance, that the dissidents were driven by a desire for publicity or fuelled by self-hate. Both these traits were referred to in an article that appeared in Israel's most popular daily newspaper, *Yediot Achronot*. Opponents of the war were equated with the 'haters of Israel', the only difference between them being their mode of operation.

> During the Black Plague in the fourteenth century, in the days of blood libels, the haters of Israel described the poisoners of wells in the following way: Wrapped in a dark cloak with a black hood on their head, they work in the middle of the night, in pitch dark, stalking between the courtyards and hiding in the alleyways until they reach the well and drop in the fatal poison ... Contemporary poisoners of the wells have adopted a new method. Not in the dark or in hiding. Exactly the opposite. The more visible it is, the more successful the poisoning. They need light, noise, a stage, an audience. They want cameras and microphones. They poison the wells in front of everybody, in bright sunlight.[35]

Those accused of stabbing the nation in the back or poisoning wells not only rejected the tone of the charges made against them, they also rejected the premises on which they were based. Thus Yossi Sarid, an Alignment Member of Knesset and one of the first politicians to oppose the invasion of Lebanon, insisted that in doing so he was fulfilling his duty as a public figure. 'Criticism after the act', Sarid argued,

> is worthless ... What is the point of finding fault after all the consequences of the war are a fait accompli? Doesn't a public figure abandon his role and betray his conscience when, during a time of difficult decisions, he postpones his criticism until later? ... Is it the duty of a public figure to express the communal mood, or to try, at least, to mould and influence it?[36]

Abba Eban, a former Alignment Member of Knesset and Foreign Minister, rejected the oft-made suggestion that opponents of the invasion were acting against the democratic norm to suspend criticism during wartime. The 'tradition' of silence was not followed for one simple reason – it does not exist.[37] And as one columnist pointed out, this is particularly so in the case of the Jewish people. 'Mutual tolerance, moderation and compromise', he reminded his readers, 'have never been the fate of the people of Israel even in the face of external danger.' Their history is characterized by fraternal strife.[38]

Critics of the war reinforced their arguments concerning 'the duty to oppose' by blaming the government for creating the dissension in the first place. Time and again they argued that Menachem Begin and his colleagues should have taken public opinion into account and stayed within the bounds of the national consensus. Failing to do so had destroyed 'our national solidarity which is based on an agreement regarding what we go to war about'.

Many of those who came out against the war drew attention to the fact that the opposition began in earnest among those who had fought in Lebanon. It was the reservists returning from the front who were the driving force of the various anti-war movements. To speak of the army being influenced by opposition politicians was, therefore, a total misreading of the situation. The protesters had been galvanized into action by their own personal experiences of the war. Aware of the gap between the declared and the real aims of the invasion, they felt an acute need to make their voices heard. They could no longer remain silent in the face of the government's distortions and half-truths.[39]

As the invasion into Lebanon became the longest war in Israel's short history, the dissent became increasingly widespread. This was particularly the case during the siege of Beirut and in the wake of the Sabra and Shatilla massacre. Long-standing opponents of the war began to point out that apolitical figures such as the President, erstwhile supporters of the government, and even some of its members had come out against the war. The Likud administration, they contended, could no longer use *ad hominem* arguments against its opponents. Many of them were clearly beyond aspersion.

Opponents of the war were at pains to point how Menachem Begin had consistently ridiculed those foreign leaders who were critical of his government's policies. Nevertheless, he and his colleagues now used these attacks in their attempt to silence domestic opposition to the war in Lebanon. To quote Abba Eban once again, 'World opinion was promoted from the stature of a negligible dwarf to that of an imposing giant.'[40] But, as he and others pointed out, the worldwide criticism was generated by the government policy rather than the opposition it engendered. In fact, the latter was beneficial to the Israeli cause. 'The protest movement constituted a counterbalance to the distorted image of the Jewish people and the Zionist enterprise, and thereby saved the good name of Israel in the eyes of the Western world.'[41]

FLESH OF OUR FLESH

While most of the opposition to the war came from political parties and extra-parliamentary groups to the left of the government, they were by no means the only ones who criticized the invasion of Lebanon. It also came under attack from the radical right. Both secular and religious advocates of a Greater Israel contended that the government had to make sure that it reaped the full benefits of the war.

Yuval Ne'eman, the chairman of the right-wing Tehiya Party, insisted that Israel not give in to international dictates and that it prepare the army for 'a lengthy and unlimited stay' in Lebanon. That was the only way, he argued, to persuade the superpowers and Syria to agree to an evacuation of all foreign forces from the Land of the Cedars, and to give time to the Christians, Druzes and Shiites to get organized. Once they had done so, it would be possible to establish a central government that was favourable towards Israel, and would be willing to include the Litani region in Israeli development programmes.[42]

Most leaders of the religious right felt that the settler movements and the State of Israel should concentrate their efforts on establishing permanent Jewish rule over the areas captured in the Six Day War. There were those, however, who adopted a more radical stance. Rav Israel Ariel of Jerusalem's Temple Institute, for instance, pointed out that southern Lebanon is part of the biblical Land of Israel and, therefore,

> We should have declared that we have no intention of leaving. We should have announced that Lebanon is flesh of our flesh like Tel Aviv and Haifa, and that we are doing this by right of the moral power granted to us by the Torah.

Going a step further, Rav Ariel attacked the government for not adopting a more aggressive stance during the course of the war, arguing that, our leaders should have entered Lebanon and Beirut immediately and without any hesitation, and killed every single one of them. Not a memory or a trace should have remained ... They should have entered Beirut at any price, without regard to the number of casualties, because we are talking about the conquest of the Land of Israel.[43]

Those who complained about unnecessary casualties were mistaken. According to the Torah, the lives of individuals must cede pride of place to the life of the community. The ends justify the means used to achieve them, however painful they may be.

ENDS AND MEANS

The invasion of Lebanon was the first Israeli military campaign that generated a serious controversy while the hostilities were still in progress. At the beginning of the war the criticism was limited to the far left of the political spectrum. However, as the invasion extended further into Lebanon and the IDF besieged and subsequently entered Beirut, the condemnation became much more widespread. Contrary to conventional wisdom, conflict with the external enemy did not lead to internal unity. Rather it deepened the divisions and highlighted the tensions in Israeli society.

The government was attacked from both sides of the political spectrum. However, although they adopted diametrically opposed stances, left and right critics alike assailed the government on the same grounds. Both groups related to the perennial issues of *jus ad bellum* and *jus in belli*. They were each concerned with the ends of the war and the means used to achieve them.

Those responsible for the conduct of the war paid little or no notice to the criticism of the radical right. They did not consider them to be a serious threat to the government. Begin and Sharon concentrated their attention instead on their opponents on the left of the political spectrum. Time and again, they questioned their right to criticize the war effort and argued that all disagreements should be shelved, at least until the fighting came to an end. However, faced with mounting opposition, Menachem Begin and his colleagues had no option but to enter the fray. They had to defend the decision to go to war and the way in which it was conducted. The government vehemently denied the allegations that the armed forces had failed to live up to the high standards of morality that characterized Israel's previous wars. Political and military leaders alike insisted that the invasion of Lebanon was no different in this respect even though the PLO deliberately positioned itself in a way that was designed to increase the number of civilian casualties. The IDF had endangered soldiers' lives in order to ensure its purity of arms.

Initially, Likud leaders justified the invasion of Lebanon by arguing that it was a war of self-defence. However, as the hostilities continued they were forced to adopt a different stance. The war, Begin and others admitted, was a war of choice but, they were at pains to point out, it was not the first of its kind. Commending their condemners, the Prime Minister and his colleagues argued that previous Labour governments had gone to war in similar circumstances. By invading Lebanon the Likud was not breaking new ground, it was simply following in the footsteps of earlier Labour administrations.

In many other contexts Menachem Begin and his colleagues tried to emphasize how they differed from their Labour predecessors. They were intent on contrasting the foreign and defence policies of the two parties and making a clear dichotomy between them. However, in light of the widespread opposition to the invasion of Lebanon, Likud leaders adopted the opposite approach. They argued that both the ends of the war and the means used to achieve them were essentially the same as those of previous ones. The emphasis was on similarity rather than differences, or continuity rather than change.

NOTES

1. The controversy about the nature of the interaction between Ariel Sharon and the Prime Minister and other members of the government during the course of the war has been examined in great detail in Shai Feldman and Heda Rechnitz-Kejner, *Deception, Concensus and War: Israel in Lebanon* (Boulder, CO: Westview Press, 1984). However, it is of only marginal importance to the present analysis and is therefore just mentioned in passing.
2. It has been suggested that the opposition parties knew the true military objectives of the invasion from the outset, but that there was a negative consensus to refrain from controversy during the first month of the war. See Gad Barzilai, *Wars, Internal Conflicts and Political Order: A Jewish Democracy in the Middle East* (Albany, NY: State University of New York Press, 1996), p. 213.
3. Yitzhak Rabin, *The Lebanon War* (Tel Aviv: Am Oved, 1983; in Hebrew), p. 33.
4. Yitzhak Rabin, 'The Price of Political Delusions', in *The Lebanon War: Between Protest and Compliance* (Tel Aviv: Hakibbutz Hameuchad, 1983; in Hebrew), p. 13.
5. *Davar*, 19 August 1982.
6. For a more comprehensive analysis of the no-choice war debate see Efraim Inbar, 'The No-Choice War Debate in Israel', *Journal of Strategic Studies* 12/1 (March 1989), pp. 22–37. The resort to this term rather than to the more usual one of a just war is explained in Aharon

Yariv, *War By Choice* (Tel Aviv: Hakibbutz Hameuchad, 1985; in Hebrew).
7. *Divrei HaKnesset* 10 (1982), pp. 27–46.
8. *Ma'ariv*, 9 July 1982.
9. This was just one example of a much wider controversy about Menachem Begin's use of the Holocaust to justify the government's foreign and defence policy. Its major contours are described on pages 114–18.
10. *Ma'ariv* and *Yediot Achronot*, 20 August 1982.
11. *Yediot Achronot*, 20 August 1982.
12. Ibid
13. *IDF Journal*, December 1982.
14. The aims and consequences of the war received widespread coverage in the national press. The different points of view have been summarized clearly and succinctly in Feldman and Rechnitz-Kijner, *Deception, Consensus and War*, pp. 3–24.
15. It was also suggested that Menachem Begin saw the war as a way to redress the image of a weak and divided Israel that he felt had been created by the evacuation of the Sinai Peninsula as part of the Camp David Accords. See for instance Nachman Raz, 'An Examination of Basics in the Light of War', in *The Political–Military Arena: An Examination and Critique of the War in Lebanon* (Ramat Efal: Yad Tabenkin, 1982; in Hebrew), p. 19.
16. Aharon Yadlin, 'A Just War. Was It Also Unpreventable?', in *The Political–Military Arena*', p. 40.
17. *Ma'ariv* and *Yediot Achronot*, 20 August 1982.
18. The Chief of Staff later claimed that the war in Lebanon had achieved all its purposes, but that the initial achievements were squandered because of Israel's failure to retain control of southern Lebanon. See Rafael Eitan, *The Story Of A Soldier* (Tel Aviv: Ma'ariv, 1985; in Hebrew), pp. 381–2.
19. Ze'ev Schiff and Ehud Ya'ari, *Israel's Lebanon War* (New York: Simon & Schuster, 1984), p. 308.
20. *Divrei HaKnesset* 94 (1982), p. 3685.
21. Ibid.
22. Many critics argued that these responses were particularly inappropriate because the massacre had occurred on the Jewish New Year and, therefore, at the beginning of the ten days of penitence that precede the Day of Atonement.
23. On certain occasions opposition spokesmen also included the Foreign Minister, Yitzhak Shamir, and referred to his involvement in the assassination of Lord Moyne, the British Resident Minister in the Middle East, during the period of the mandate.
24. In certain instances government critics also engaged in self-criticism. They blamed themselves for not taking strident enough action against the Likud administration in general and the invasion of Lebanon in particular. 'I am guilty', one columnist wrote, 'because I spoke but did not repeat myself, because I spoke but did not shout, and because I shouted but did nothing to stop the actions that were carried out in my name.'
25. The historian, Anita Shapira, expressed concern that this kind of dichotomization would prepare the ground for the massacre of Jews who had criticized the government and been denounced as traitors.
26. Hanan Hever and Moshe Ron, *Fighting and Killing Without End: Political Poetry in the Lebanon War* (Tel Aviv: Kibbutz Hameuchad, 1983; in Hebrew), p. 68.
27. Government critics tried to drive this message home by drawing attention to Menachem Begin's proclivity for demanding the establishment of committees of inquiry while leader of the opposition, and his decision to set one up to investigate the murder of Chaim Arlosoroff. The controversy that this commission caused is discussed on pages 118–21.
28. *Ma'ariv*, 20 September 1982.
29. Nurith Gertz, *Capture of a Dream: National Myths in Israeli Culture* (Tel Aviv: Am Oved, 1995; in Hebrew), pp. 101–2.
30. Their justification was based, to a large extent at least, on the alleged tendency of Likud leaders to identify government and state, and to 'demonize political enemies'. These allegations are discussed in Chapter 5. See in particular pages 67–71.
31. Eitan, *Story of a Soldier*, p. 304.
32. During the controversy about the Sabra and Shatilla massacre, Likud leaders often drew

attention to Shimon Peres' attempts to persuade Ezer Weizman to leave the Likud and join forces in the establishment of an alternative government.

33. Opposition leaders responded by pointing out that this was not particularly commendable because he supported all the wars that had taken place whilst the Labour Party was in power.
34. Opponents of the war also resorted to this kind of argumentation. They explained the lack of dissent in terms of obedience to authority, conformity to social pressure, and other psychological phenomena. See for instance Uri Levitan, 'Four Psychological Phenomena and the War in Lebanon', in Rubik Rosenthal (ed.), *Lebanon: the Other War* (Tel Aviv: Sifriat Hapoalim, 1983; in Hebrew), pp. 145–54.
35. *Yediot Achronot*, 25 June 1982.
36. *Ha'aretz*, 25 June 1982.
37. Abba Eban, 'The Duty to Oppose', in Hillel Schenker (ed.), *After Lebanon: The Israeli–Palestinian Connection* (New York: Pilgrim Press, 1983), p. 365.
38. *Ma'ariv*, 1 October 1982.
39. There were, however, differences of opinion as to what form the protest should take. In particular, many opponents of the war objected to the 'There is a Limit' movement which advocated refusing to do military service in Lebanon. There were also serious disagreements as to whether and/or how those serving in the regular army should express their opposition to the war. On both these issues see Ruth Linn, *Not Shooting and Not Crying: Psychological Inquiry into Moral Disobedience* (Westport, CT: Greenwood, 1989).
40. Eban, 'Duty to Oppose', p. 369.
41. Yehoshua Arieli, 'Israeli Democracy Facing the Test of the War in Lebanon', in Rubik Rosenthal (ed.), *Lebanon: The Other War*, p. 177 (in Hebrew).
42. Yuval Ne'eman, *A Sober Policy?* (Ramat Gan: Revivim, 1984; in Hebrew), pp. 111–13.
43. These quotations are taken from an interview on the local radio station, the Voice of Tel Aviv. They appeared under the title 'Not to Leave a Trace' in the journal of the Council of Settlements in Judea, Samaria and Gaza, *Nekuda*, 12 November 1980.

5

Verbal Violence

VIOLENCE ON THE STREETS

Until the upheaval in 1977, Israeli elections were always regarded as a foregone conclusion. Only after the Likud broke the stalemate and assumed the reins of power did people realize that things could be different, and that they could go either way. This new situation found its clearest expression in the changing fortunes of the two major parties during the election campaign for the tenth Knesset four years later.

The Alignment's initial 30 per cent lead in the public opinion polls at the start of the campaign was gradually whittled away, and by the beginning of June the Likud had drawn ahead. However, the turnabout proved to be rather short-lived. During the last month of the campaign the Alignment recovered and the pre-election polls predicted a tie. On this occasion at least, they were proved right. Only 10,000 votes, 0.5 per cent of those cast, separated the two major parties. It was the closest race ever.

The 1982 election was also characterized by a particularly high correlation between ethnic background and voting preferences. As has already been pointed out, two-thirds of Likud supporters were of Eastern (North African or Asian) origin, and 70 per cent of those who chose the Alignment were from a Western (European or American) background. The polarizing effect of this dichotomy was intensified by the high correlation between ethnicity and three other important variables: class, religion and political ideology. Likud voters tended to belong to a lower socioeconomic class, were more likely to be religiously observant or traditional in outlook, and had more right-wing political views than Alignment supporters. The elections therefore pitted two fundamentally different blocs against each other.

This unprecedented competitiveness and polarization led to the most violent election campaign in Israeli history.[1] The problem first appeared at the end of April when Shimon Peres, the Alignment Prime Ministerial candidate, was pelted with tomatoes during a visit to the traditional post-Passover Mimouna celebrations, and it reached a peak during the last month of the campaign. June was marred by disturbances at opposition rallies, the burning of the local party headquarters, attacks on cars bearing Alignment stickers, and on people wearing party T-shirts. Hardly a day went by without a violent incident of one kind or another.[2] The late comeback of the Alignment was, to a large extent at least, a reaction against these attacks, because public attention focused on the political leaders who allegedly incited the violence rather than on their followers who engaged in it. Clearly, therefore, the violence was not just an unfortunate consequence of the elections, it was also one of the major influences on its outcome.

The new Likud-led administration was markedly more right-wing than its predecessor. Both the government's increasingly aggressive settlement policy and the continuing war in Lebanon met with a great deal of criticism. They exacerbated the already deep divisions within Israeli society. With the publication of the Kahan Report these tensions once again erupted into violence on the streets. Peace Now organized a rally to try and force the government's hand regarding Ariel Sharon's dismissal from the government. It was meant to take the form of a peaceful march from Zion Square, in Jerusalem's downtown commercial centre, to the Prime Minister's office, about a mile away. From the outset, however, the rally was marred by violence.

According to the 'testimony' of Shulamit Hareven, a prominent novelist and newspaper columnist, and one of the leaders of the march:

> Right from the start, when the demonstrators set out ... they sensed that this was no ordinary clash of ideas. What was in the air was not the familiar level of marginal violence. Even before the Peace Now supporters arrived, an organized group of violent hooligans had gathered ... All along the route, they broke into the lines of marchers with great force, shouting, whistling and punching them. Despite the fists, the blows, and the curses, the march moves forward ... The marchers show restraint. They are not hitting back. The almost overwhelming feeling that we share today is that the street is on the verge of civil war, and that has to be stopped at any price ... Democracy has some strange faces at this time. To stand under a shower of spit seems to be one of them.[3]

But all this was just a prelude. The real drama took place after the march came to an end. As the demonstrators began to disperse, somebody threw a grenade into the crowd killing one person and injuring ten others. Emil Greenzweig became 'the first fatality of a political demonstration in Israel'. However, even this tragic event did not lead to a cooling of tempers. The anti-Peace Now demonstrators continued to curse and disturb the marchers as they brought the victims of the grenade attack to the hospital emergency room. Ariel Sharon's supporters meted out similar treatment to those who came to Emil's funeral and/or participated in the memorial vigil during the traditional week of mourning. As far as they were concerned, it was business as usual.

It took almost a year before Greenzweig's assailant was apprehended.[4] However, this delay did not prevent politicians and publicists of all persuasions from making assumptions about the kind of person or persons who carried out the grenade attack and, even more importantly, about those who had led him to do so. In this case, as in that of the election violence, attention focused on the perpetrators of the violence rather than on their alleged auxiliaries.

THE HANDS ARE THE HANDS OF ESAU

Throughout the 1981 election campaign, Alignment leaders and the two party-affiliated newspapers, *Davar* and *Al Hamishmar*, emphasized the seriousness of the violence by describing specific incidents, drawing attention to their increasing severity, and giving up-to-date statistics of the number of attacks that had occurred. These reports of the existing situation were accompanied by predictions about what might happen in the future. The violence, it was feared, would become more extreme during the course of the campaign, and continue after the elections.

The killing of Emil Greenzweig confirmed people's worst fears. Their prophecies of doom were, it seemed, coming true. In contrast to the oft-made contention that the latest trauma blots out the memory of previous ones, many observers made a causal connection between them. They drew attention to the steady deterioration in the behaviour of the mob and argued that the attacks against property had led to assaults on individuals and, in turn, to 'the first victim of internal terror'. But the worst, they feared, was still to come. The fatal grenade attack had 'broken a barrier' and it could therefore lead to even worse violence in the future. The threat of assassinations of leftist politicians and a civil war was more real than ever.

The Likud supporters who engaged in violence during the election campaign were sometimes portrayed as 'mercenaries' who attacked Alignment property and persons because they were paid to do so. On other occasions they were depicted as 'people who are mentally abnormal and whose only cure is to be found on the psychiatrist's couch'. The two images, however, had one other important feature in common. They both suggested that the perpetrators of violence were apolitical animals who were driven by other considerations.

Alignment spokesmen most frequently referred to their assailants as hooligans or ruffians who were simply expressing their frustrations with Israeli society. The setting does not matter, so violence breaks out whenever and wherever the mob gets together. During the soccer season they let off steam at the local stadium, and when there are elections they give vent to their feelings at Alignment rallies.[5] Crowd psychology rather than political ideology is the major cause of violence.

The Alignment-affiliated newspapers took this argument a step further. Reporters and columnists repeatedly referred to those who engaged in violence as savages or barbarians. So too did the cartoonists. In Figure 1, the Likud trio is standing outside the Alignment office and their leader is telling them to get ready for battle because he smells humans.[6] Thus, those who resorted to violence were not simply denied the recognition accorded to political actors. In many instances, their most basic status as human beings was impugned.

Participants in the anti-Peace Now demonstration were thought to be from a similar background to those who engaged in violence during the election campaign. Consequently, they were portrayed in essentially the same way. Although no mention was made of mercenaries on this occasion, the more violent Likud supporters were once again referred to as crazies and/or criminals. To quote one reporter who claimed to be well versed in such matters:

> My colleagues and I know many people from the world of crime who think they have a monopoly on patriotism ... Whenever they have the opportunity, they put on a cloak of pure and refined patriotism and unleash their tongues and their fists against those whom they consider to be traitors or enemies of the state. Each one by himself is not a great hero, but when they get together as a mob they can stand up against the country's best fighters and scream: traitors.[7]

Figure 1: Davar cartoon depicting the Likud as savages standing outside the Alignment office. Their leader tells them to prepare for battle because he can smell humans.

Opposition leaders and supporters also returned to the dehumanization of their violent opponents. In addition to referring to 'the mob' as barbarians and savages, they compared it to particular primitive tribes and to different beasts of prey. In contrast to Emil Greenzweig, who represented beautiful Israel, the person who killed him and injured the other marchers personified the animality of the Jewish state.

Both the hooligan and the barbarian image drew attention to what was considered to be the major characteristic of those who resorted to violence – a low level of self-restraint. This trait, together with the proclivity of crowds to become a violent entity, made them easy prey for the oratory of their revered leader, 'Begin, the king of Israel'.

THE VOICE IS THE VOICE OF JACOB

Throughout the election, Alignment leaders insisted that the violence directed against them was organized by the Likud. They claimed that, besides being paid for their efforts, those involved were bussed to the party's rallies, furnished with appropriate placards, and given detailed instructions on how to behave or, to be more precise, to misbehave. In certain instances, Alignment campaign managers blamed the local Likud functionaries, but more often they pointed an accusing finger at national leaders. They were in overall charge of the campaign and therefore responsible for its violent turn.

Significantly, however, this was not the major Alignment indictment of the Likud. Indeed, many party leaders were of the opinion that the violence was not officially organized at either the national or the local level. Rather, they blamed the Likud in general, and Menachem Begin in particular, for creating an atmosphere that legitimated the attacks on Alignment property and persons. Their failure to take effective action against violence, and their only thinly veiled encouragement of it, was the root of the problem. 'There is no need to give explicit instructions in order to activate the masses or incite hooligans', a Davar editorial insisted. 'The indirect incitement of passions, and calming people down at the same time as encouraging them to raise their fists, is enough.'[8]

Menachem Begin bore the brunt of the Alignment attack. Time and again he was criticized for his rabble-rousing and demagoguery.[9] It was the Prime Minister's verbal violence, Shimon Peres and other opposition leaders argued, that led to the physical violence against them.[10] The attacks on Alignment property and persons were simply 'the ugly translation of Begin's words into the language of the street'. This point was often driven home by juxtaposing photographs of the Prime Minister addressing Likud rallies with those depicting his more volatile supporters. The message was clear: Begin's words led to their deeds.

Alignment leaders made a similar argument after the killing of Emil Greenzweig. Shimon Peres, for instance, summed up the process as follows: 'The first person throws out a word, the second throws a tomato, the third throws a stone and the fourth throws a grenade.'[11] This time, however, the focus of criticism shifted from Begin to Ariel Sharon. He was severely castigated for his denigration of the Kahan Report, and particularly for his public statement that it had 'stamped Israel with the mark of Cain'. The morning after the grenade attack the *Davar* editorial made an analogy to the biblical story of Jacob and Esau. 'The hands are the hands of the person who threw the grenade,' it declared, 'but the voice is the voice of Ariel Sharon.'[12]

Time and again, Alignment leaders drew attention to the 'lexicon of incitement' used against them and, for that matter, against all those who disagreed with the government's policy regarding the occupied territories. They protested that anyone opposing the idea of a Greater Israel was immediately branded as a traitor, foreign agent, fifth columnist or, in local terms, an Ashafist.[13] The epithet used was, of course, immaterial because they all conveyed the same message: that anybody in favour of territorial compromise was betraying the country, and siding with its most virulent enemy.

The constant accusations of 'stabbing the nation in the back' were attributed to a tendency on the part of Menachem Begin and his colleagues to identify the government with the state. This allegedly led to the 'demonization of political enemies' and, in turn, to the legitimation of the use of violence against them.[14] To quote a lead article in the Mapam daily, *Al Hamishmar*,

> There is an iron logic in this madness ... a king is someone whose actions one does not question. One does not dare to doubt his judgement, and it does not cross anyone's mind to examine his decisions. The king is the law ... and he rules. Anybody who dares to think, to question, or to protest, is clearly a bleeding-heart Ashkenazi, a pursuer of peace, and a traitorous and cursed agent of the PLO ... Those who sally forth with such satisfaction at public rallies chanting 'King of Israel', those who stigmatize anyone who dares to hold them to account ... are responsible for the attacks on Jewish victims in the civil war ... They are not the result of fate, but the fruit of human action. They have an address, and someone is responsible for them.[15]

Menachem Begin's demagoguery on these issues was thought to have led to a release of 'primitive passions' amongst his supporters. This was especially the case when those who had 'a low provocation threshold' became part of 'an excited mass'. The combination of Begin's rhetorical skills, the susceptibility of his followers, and the dynamics of crowd behaviour was considered to be a particularly explosive one. According to many, it made the violence on the streets almost inevitable, regardless of whether or not the Prime Minister and his campaign managers wanted it to happen.

Paradoxically, Menachem Begin the all-powerful orator was sometimes portrayed as having lost control of the situation. The mob had gone further than he expected. It had become 'a golem that rose up against its creator'. In a number of instances this argument was taken a step further and the relationship between 'Begin, the king of Israel' and his followers was depicted as mutually reinforcing. Thus, according to one political correspondent first 'the mass of incited admirers translates Begin's demagoguery into the language of wild violence' then 'the tables are turned and the mob begins to control him. Begin is mesmerized by his own oratory. It's like a life-giving drug that baffles the senses.'[16]

Alignment leaders admitted that some party spokesmen engaged in verbal violence, but they were always at pains to point out that it was much less extreme than that of the Likud.[17] In the words of one member of the Knesset, Yossi Sarid:

> The difference is very simple ... Even when we engage in fierce debate, we never deny the other side's legitimacy. We never deny the integrity of the rival opinion, even though we are convinced that it is disastrous for the State of Israel. We accept that that is what you really believe ... But you do not say that that is what we think, and that we are mistaken. You say that we are insincere, that we are foreign allies or agents, that we are traitors.[18]

The Alignment therefore rejected Likud proposals for a joint committee during the election campaign, and a framework for consultations between the Prime Minister and the leader of the opposition after the killing of Emil Greenzweig. Setting up such bodies, Shimon Peres and his colleagues argued, would give the impression that the Alignment and the Likud were equally responsible for the situation when, in fact, only the latter was to blame. 'It takes a great deal of impudence to come up with such ideas', an *Al Hamishmar* editorial noted. 'It's like suggesting the establishment of a coordinating committee between the attacker and the attacked, the rapist and the raped, or the robber and his victim.'[19]

Rather than agreeing to bipartisan action, Alignment leaders entreated Menachem Begin to use his immense political authority and notorious rhetorical ability to 'put an end to inflamed passions'. Only he, they felt, stood a chance of convincing the more rabid Likud supporters of the need for greater tolerance. Having successfully demonized the critics of a Greater Israel, Menachem Begin had to rehabilitate them by explaining that they were merely political opponents and not enemies of the state. However, his half-hearted denunciation of the violence convinced the Alignment that the Prime Minister was unwilling to do so.

This pessimistic reading of the situation led to a debate about whether the opponents of the government should take the law into their own hands. Those in favour of doing so claimed that it was wrong to turn the other cheek because perpetrators of violence understood only the language of force. Thus the playwright, Yehoshua Sobol. offered the following diagnosis of 'the sickness and how it should be treated'.

> Nice words and self-restraint will not change the situation ... the ideology of the animals that do this kind of thing should be regarded as merely a thin layer of justification which they seem to need for one reason or another ... In fact, however, they are simply sadists. Sadists are people who interpret any kind of restraint as weakness, and this, more than anything else, eggs them on ... It is therefore necessary to respond forcefully to the sadism of hooligans and the mob ... The time has come to treat them for their sickness, and not according to some lofty ideals that only serve to intensify their ailment.[20]

In contrast, the opponents of such partisan action insisted that the Alignment and Peace Now should under no circumstances 'descend to the level of the Likud'. To do so would simply play into the hands of the hooligans. Thus, at the height of the election campaign Shimon Peres made a public appeal to his supporters to exercise self-restraint. It is, he argued, the last bastion against the decline of the country into total chaos. And, in a similar vein, Peace Now urged its members to 'control their anger and not be drawn into a civil war'. That was the most appropriate way of honouring the memory of Emil Greenzweig.

CAN THE ETHIOPIAN CHANGE HIS SKIN?

On the basis of their claim that it was verbal violence that led to the violence in the streets, Alignment leaders concentrated their attack on Menachem Begin and Ariel Sharon rather than on their more volatile supporters. With regard to the Prime Minister, opposition spokesmen tried to drive this message home by placing his rabble-rousing in a much wider perspective. It was, they argued, part of a more general pattern.

Time and again, Alignment leaders lambasted Begin for his undiplomatic comments both to and about various world leaders. They quoted his uncomplimentary remarks on Valéry Giscard d'Estaing, the former president of France, Chancellor Helmut Schmidt of West Germany and

US Secretary of Defense Casper Weinberger, amongst others, and drew attention to their deleterious effect on Israel's relationship with its allies. In addition, Begin's constant resort to Balaam's description of Israel as 'a people that dwells alone' in support of the government's foreign policy turned into a self-fulfilling prophecy. Even Israel's closest friends had distanced themselves from the Likud government and left it completely isolated in the international arena. Now, Alignment leaders lamented, the whole world is indeed against us.

During the 1981 campaign Begin's demagoguery was often portrayed as a long-standing phenomenon. One Alignment advertisement, for instance, quoted a speech made by David Ben-Gurion 25 years earlier in which he criticized Menachem Begin for his way with words. 'Ever since the days of ancient Athens', he argued,

> there have been two kinds of leaders in democracies – the demagogue and the statesman. The path of the demagogue is a simple one. There is nothing beyond his power. There is no land that he cannot conquer, no enemy he is unable to destroy, no desire of the public that he cannot fulfil, and no instinct of the masses that he is unable to satisfy, because his power is in his words. He is an orator and there are no constraints on his language.

In order to drive this message home, Alignment leaders recalled Menachem Begin's vitriolic remarks about his opponents both within his own party and beyond its ranks. Of particular importance to this study, however, are the references to past instances in which Begin incited his supporters and encouraged their resort to violence. The most recent one was the anti-Kissinger demonstrations during the post-Yom Kippur War negotiations for an interim peace agreement with Egypt. However, the most frequently mentioned incident was the mass rally against German reparations in January 1952. According to another election advertisement,

> It wasn't by the rioters' initiative that they reached the Knesset esplanade. They had been organized and transported to Jerusalem from all over Israel. A short while earlier you had stood on a platform in Zion Square. You whetted your followers' appetites and voiced the terrible cry: 'This will be a war of life or death. Today I'll give the order, blood!' Nearly thirty years have passed since that chilling event but it turns out that you haven't changed ... You remain what you have always been ... One and

all recognize the pictures of things before us these days. One thread binds them to the 1952 riots and the scenes of political violence. You, MENACHEM BEGIN. *Victims have come and gone since then. But you, head agitator, have remained.* [Capitals and italics in original.]

Menachem Begin was now Prime Minister and responsible for law and order, but he continued in his old ways. Invoking the prophet Jeremiah (13:23), one Alignment leader asked, 'Can the Ethiopian change his skin or the leopard its spots?'

This composite picture of Menachem Begin, or what Shimon Peres disparagingly referred to as 'Beginism', was augmented by comparisons to other political leaders. In order to emphasize the dangers of verbal violence, the Alignment campaign managers drew a series of analogies between the situation in Israel and those in Argentina, Libya and, above all, Iran. Begin's followers were frequently referred to as 'Khomeinists' and he himself was likened to the ayatollah, as in the following advertisement:

> In Iran the incited mass hail the elderly leader who vilifies the entire world while the national economy is in ruins and the country is more isolated than ever in the international arena. Under his direct inspiration or with his silent approval fanatics are trying to stifle the voices of the moderates. Scary, no?

During the election campaign both *Davar* and *Al Hamishmar* carried a number of articles comparing the current situation in Israel with Italy and Germany before the rise of fascism and Nazism.[21] They drew attention to three areas of similarity: socioeconomic conditions such as galloping inflation, rising unemployment and internal unrest, the exploitation of tensions with neighbouring countries in order to foster national chauvinism, and the lack of any resolute action to prevent a fascist takeover of power by democratic means. In Israel, as in Europe, opponents of the regime denied the gravity of the threat. So, Alignment supporters warned, 'don't say that it can't happen here, because it has already happened in more cultured countries'.

Similar arguments were used after the killing of Emil Greenzweig. Time and again, politicians and publicists contended that 'the historical parallels are abundantly clear to anyone who has eyes in his head'. Referring to the government as fascist is therefore not a form of verbal violence. It is permissible and even obligatory to draw attention to the 'monopolization of patriotism'[22] and other fascist trends in Israeli society, and to fight against them. 'History', one columnist in the independent daily *Ha'aretz* pointed out, 'does not repeat itself. Only the tests do, and people know or do not know how to pass them.'[23]

SPILLING THE BLOOD

Accusing Menachem Begin and his colleagues of engaging in verbal violence was by no means the only way in which opposition leaders blamed the government for the attacks on Alignment property and persons, and the killing of Emil Greenzweig. There were other reasons why the government could and, for that matter, should be held responsible for the violence on the streets. Ever since assuming the reins of power in 1977 the Likud had been guilty of a whole series of sins of omission and commission in this regard.

Many observers drew attention to the violent actions of Jewish settlers in the occupied territories. In doing so, however, they tended to focus on the response or, to be more precise, the lack of response of the law enforcement agencies rather than the illegal acts themselves. Shortly after the Greenzweig killing, for instance, Mordechai Virshuvsky, a member of Knesset for the self-defined centrist party, Shinui, recalled that,

> for weeks and months we, the citizens of the State of Israel saw the heroes of Yamit [who were forced to evacuate as part of the Israel–Egypt peace agreement] say that they would break the law, and refuse to leave or to be ejected ... Not only was no action taken against them; they were regarded as people who experienced the pains of the motherland more acutely than others ... The government did nothing until the last minute, until there was absolutely no choice. This evoked a feeling amongst the public that some things are above the law, and that violence sometimes pays ... Once this happens, violence not only becomes permissible, it even generates sympathy. In this way we gradually weaken the rule of law.[24]

The Likud-led government was also criticized for failing to take the requisite preventive and punitive action against settlers who engaged in violence against the local Arab population. Hence the frequent reference to the failure of the police to apprehend those responsible for the bombing attacks on five West Bank mayors in June 1980.[25] Time and again, opposition spokesmen pointed out that 'the Green Line only exists on paper, not in real life'. The moment that 'spilling blood in one place is permissible, all restrictions are eradicated'. Murder knows no borders.

A number of the government's opponents took this argument a step further. They contended that violence on the streets was not only due to the lack of official response to the violence of the settlers; it was also attributable to the government's own use of force in the occupied territories and in Lebanon. Yossi Sarid, for instance, argued that,

> Those who thought that it was possible to turn a blind eye to injustice on the other side of the Green Line, and remain sensitive to iniquity on this side, were mistaken. Those who thought we could gradually become corrupt on the West Bank, and retain our innocence here, were wrong. Those who thought that it was possible to belittle the value of a human being there, without the same thing happening here, were mistaken ... members of the Knesset, is there anybody who thinks that a state which knocks on doors in the middle of the night there, will not act similarly in other places? Maybe it was possible to believe that in 1967 when we spoke about an 'enlightened occupation' ... but can you still do so now, with everything that is going on?[26]

The historian, Shlomo Ben-Ami, tried to drive this message home by referring to the experience of other countries. Writing in *Al Hamishmar*, he drew attention to the fact that no regime had managed to control a large national minority and remain democratic. Ben-Ami suggested that not only was Israel unlikely to be an exception to this 'iron rule'; the lack of physical distance between the occupier and the occupied, and the fact that the relationship between them was based on mystical rather than rational grounds, made the demise of democracy even more likely than elsewhere.[27]

In the same issue, Michael Hersogar placed the government's actions in a more local historical context. He traced the Likud administration's policy in the occupied territories and its tolerance of the use of violence by non-state actors to Revisionist attitudes during the period of the Yishuv. He contended that they derived from the movement's militant approach towards the problem of Arab terror and its disregard of democratically elected institutions. Current attitudes towards the use of violence were nothing new, they were just more of the same.[28]

AND YOU SHALL CHOOSE LIFE

The deep grief and widespread mourning in the wake of the killing of Emil Greenzweig was attributed to the fact that 'it symbolized the destruction of the best in our country by the nation's worst elements'. Thus, the Peace Now press statement released immediately after the grenade attack expressed the movement's determination to continue the struggle, because it is for the very existence of a sane and democratic society in Israel.[29] Subsequently, politicians and publicists alike referred to the conflict as a clash between two irreconcilable cultures. For some, it was a battle between two diametrically opposed but legitimate visions of Zionism. For others, the other camp was clearly beyond the pale. As Shulamit Hareven put it in the wake of the Greenzweig killing:

> If there are still people who believe that we are fighting against a different but legitimate point of view or against differences of opinion that are acceptable within a democracy, last night made them realize that they were mistaken. We are fighting, literally, against fascism. If the government will not control its hot-tempered supporters, it will bear responsibility for whatever happens.[30]

Not surprisingly, this dichotomization into two warring camps was particularly marked during the election campaign. Alignment leaders frequently drew attention to the fateful nature of the choice facing the country. The election was not simply a contest between two parties or even two policies, but rather a clash between two worldviews. Alignment supporters were therefore urged to overlook the faults of their own party, and forget the differences of opinion between them. All efforts had to be directed against the Likud because 'the campaign is about our entire future. It is a matter of all or nothing.'

The image of the elections as a struggle for the 'soul of the land' found its clearest expression in a series of articles by two of Israel's most prominent novelists, S. Yizhar and Amos Oz. Sometimes they portrayed the campaign as the latest round in the perennial struggle between Labour and Revisionist Zionism. On other occasions they referred to it as a choice between statehood and exile. The essential message was that Israel had to recapture the spirit of yesteryear. Thus, in one of his letters to a young voter, Oz wrote as follows:

> In songs and slogans they try to persuade us to continue moving forward. Forward to what? Forward to political and military adventures, arrogant

prattle and empty gestures. Forward to the annexation of more than a million Palestinian Arabs as a result of which Israel will cease to be a Jewish state. Forward to the destruction of the social and economic structure by mass bribery and the encouragement of profiteering. Forward to ethnic incitement and hatred. Forward to religious coercion in all realms of life. Forward to the ghetto. But this time you have to choose. The time has come to go a little backwards. To return to the movements of building and creation. To return to political moderation, tolerance and vision. To return to the joy of Zionist fulfillment, to the field and workshop, to the building of the land. To return to the most beautiful years of our lives, the years of creation and growth. To return from the ghetto to the Land of Israel.[31]

Significantly, this struggle over the future of Israeli society often revolved around the issue of violence. It became a summary symbol of the clash between the two major parties. Some Alignment advertisements contended that voters had to choose 'between hooliganism and Zionism'. Others referred to the problem as a symptom of 'the battle between two civilizations, one constructive the other destructive'. The choice, they insisted, was 'between life and death'.

One of the Likud's major advertisements showed a map of the settlements that had been established on both sides of the Green Line during the party's four years in power. The accompanying text claimed that Menachem Begin's government had thereby 'prevented a lament for generations. The Israeli response that has proven itself over the last hundred years is Jewish settlement! We are on the map. This map cannot be reversed.' The Alignment responded by questioning the Likud's accomplishments and drawing attention to their own achievements in this regard. Election advertisements contended that while many of the settlements established by the Likud were temporary or had already been abandoned, those founded by earlier Labour administrations 'are there come rain or shine, and not just before the elections'. Of particular interest in this study, however, is the way in which the Alignment used the settlement map as one of the motifs in its critique of Menachem Begin's demagoguery (see Figure 2). Under the caption, 'The Likud is on the map, the map of violence', it listed those places where there had been attacks on Alignment property and persons, and referred once again to the two alternatives facing the country. 'This time you really have to choose between Beginism and an enlightened government.'

Figure 2: 'The Likud is on the map, the map of violence.' An Alignment election advertising poster using the settlement map as a motif in its critique of Menachem Begin's demagoguery.

VERBAL VIOLENCE

This stark choice was perhaps most graphically illustrated in the advertisement shown in Figure 3. It reads as follows: 'Begin be warned, Shimon Peres is waiting for you. You represent those who throw tomatoes. He represents those who grow them, and they are still the majority.' Thus, the projectiles that were tossed at the beginning of the campaign came to represent its major theme: the struggle between those who had built the Jewish state and those who were allegedly destroying it.

LET HIM SEARCH HIS OWN DEEDS

Violence was one of the major issues during the last stages of the election campaign and, as has already been pointed out, it was widely regarded as the primary cause of the Likud's declining fortunes in the public opinion polls. Not surprisingly, therefore, party leaders did their utmost to play down the problem by claiming that even the most serious incidents were no more than 'minor disturbances'. They also rejected the allegation of having encouraged the attacks on Alignment

Figure 3: 'Begin be warned, Shimon Peres is waiting for you. You represent those who throw tomatoes. He represents those who grow them, and they are still the majority.' An election campaign advertising poster illustrating the choice between Beginism and an enlightened government.

property and persons. In fact, exactly the opposite was the case. Menachem Begin and other members of the government had done everything within their power to discourage the resort to violence, and had roundly condemned those who did so.

The Likud also rejected the allegations concerning Menachem Begin's oratory in the past. Election advertisements claimed that he had always been a loyal opposition leader, and drew attention to the fact that he had agreed to join the National Unity government before the Six Day War. Moving further back into the past, Likud spokesmen also recalled Begin's restraint during the armed struggle against the British mandate and the subsequent breaking up of the underground movements. Throughout his career, they argued, he had tried to emphasize the common ground between the different strands of Zionism, and to use his oratorical skills to that end.

Party leaders defended themselves by denigrating those who resorted to violence during the election campaign and at the anti-Peace Now demonstrations. Leaving the Prime Minister's office after the grenade attack, Ariel Sharon condemned 'the maniac or the maniacs' who had thrown the grenade minutes earlier. Other party leaders adopted a similar stance, or suggested that the killer was criminally motivated. While there were those who accepted the possibility that the attack had been carried out for political reasons, they insisted that the perpetrator was part of a hot-headed fringe and in no way representative of the party rank and file.[32]

Likud campaign managers also went on the offensive. They claimed that the Alignment's 'special unit for spreading lies and planting fabrications' had exaggerated the problem because the opposition did not have a serious political platform. The party's supporters were therefore urged 'to stand firm and not be influenced by enemy provocations that are designed to heat up the atmosphere'. Doing so would only play into Shimon Peres' hands by enhancing his chances of winning the elections.

After the killing of Emil Greenzweig, Menachem Begin and his colleagues took this argument a step further and accused the Alignment of engaging in a blood libel. As in the case of Chaim Arlosoroff, 50 years earlier, they attributed the murder to right-wing incitement, even though there was no evidence whatsoever to that effect. Not surprisingly, therefore, when Yona Avrushmi was arrested a year later, on suspicion of having thrown the fatal grenade, the Likud leaders enjoined their opposition counterparts to make a public confession and ask their forgiveness. His criminal record and lack of affiliation to any right-wing organization were clear indications of the fact that the murder was not politically motivated.[33]

In both cases of violence, the Alignment was not only held to task for its post-facto exaggerations and fabrications of the role of the Likud, it was also accused of having caused the violence in the first place. On a number of occasions, Menachem Begin and his colleagues claimed that the attacks on Alignment property and persons, and the Peace Now demonstration were just a response to prior violence of the left.[34] In other instances, they attributed the violence on the streets to the negative record of the various Labour administrations. Thus, after the throwing of tomatoes at Shimon Peres at the beginning of the election campaign, a Likud campaign manager declared that Alignment leaders should 'examine their record during 29 years in power and draw the appropriate conclusions, rather than blame the negative reaction to them on others'.[35] Invariably, however, Likud leaders, in common with their Alignment counterparts, drew attention to the perils of verbal violence. They emphasized the power of words rather than deeds.

Government spokesmen often drew attention to the detrimental effects of opposition remarks about its supporters. Referring to the Likud rank and file as a mob just encouraged them to behave like one, and labels such as fascist and Khomeinists[36] made them even more prone to violence. Statements sympathetic to the Palestinians were thought to have a similar effect. Thus Elyakim Ha'ezni, one of the most prominent and scathing right-wing publicists, declared:

> Public expression of understanding and support for the enemy during the course of a war is itself a form of violence. It is, in fact, this kind of violence that gave rise to the disturbances at meetings and demonstrations of the left. They are attributable to the provocation of the 'peace camp' and not to the actions of other parties or of the government.[37]

In a series of interviews in the press and on radio and television, Geula Cohen, a member of the Knesset for the right-wing Techiya party, criticized members of the Israeli left for speaking a 'beautiful Hebrew' that degraded those who were less well-educated, and destroyed their self-respect. She felt that this mode of speech, although very different to the epithets used to describe the Likud's more rabid supporters, had exactly the same effect. As part of a more general 'violence of condescension' it precluded the possibility of real dialogue, and therefore led to a steady worsening of the relations between the rival camps.[38] Her argument was subsequently developed by a one-time contributor to *Ha'aretz*. 'Nowadays', Chaim Hacham wrote,

> violence is not necessarily expressed physically or verbally ... The real violence is found in haughtiness and pride. An entire camp believes that it is more equal, more peace-loving, more democratic, and the sole representative of 'beautiful Israel'. When they take to the streets they are demonstrating; when others do so, they are hooligans ... The verbal and physical violence will only come to an end when a democratic, legitimate, public debate begins on the same rather than on different levels. It is impossible when one side talks as if it is sitting on a dais, and the other side, the guilty one, sits below, defending itself the whole time. Only when we stop talking in terms of superiority and inferiority will we return to the kind of debate that is essential in every democratic country.[39]

Given the stridency of the Likud counterattack and the unwillingness of party leaders to accept responsibility for the violence on the streets, their proposals for dealing with the problem were surprisingly balanced. They pointed to the need for leaders on both sides of the political spectrum to set an example from above. Opening the Knesset debate on 'the criminal act of throwing the grenade outside the Prime Minister's office', Speaker of the Knesset, Menachem Savidor called on members to provide 'a model of tolerance and mutual respect, despite the differences of opinion between them'.[40] In a similar vein, Likud member Ronnie Milo proposed the establishment of a framework for consultations between the Prime Minister and the leader of the opposition. By engaging in a dialogue of this nature, he argued, the two parties would send a clear message to their followers – that one can disagree and still respect the other's point of view.

The importance of the example set by those at the helm did not obviate the need for dealing with the problem at the grass-roots level. The school system was widely regarded as being particularly important in this respect. Thus, after the killing of Emil Greenzweig, the deputy Director General of the Ministry of Education called upon teachers to discuss the grenade attack and condemn it unequivocally, to point out the dangers inherent in verbal violence, and to explain the need to respect opposing points of view. In this instance at least, children had to be taught not to follow the example of their elders.

These proposals were backed up by frequent reference to the talmudic statement that the second temple was destroyed as a punishment for groundless hatred, and to the folk wisdom that the third temple will only be built when the Jewish people make up for their past misdeeds and engage in 'love for its own sake'. Everybody from the left and the right therefore had to comply with the twofold biblical commandment 'not to hate your brother in your heart', and 'to love your neighbour as yourself'.

WHERE THERE IS NO VISION

The discussion until now has focused on the stance of the two largest parties – the Likud and the Alignment – on the violence that occurred during the 1981 election campaign and after the publication of the Kahan Report. This is not to suggest, however, that they were the only participants in these controversies. Ultra-orthodox/Haredi leaders,[41] for instance, also took an active part in both debates. As far as they were concerned, secular Zionism in general rather than one particular variant of it was to blame for the upsurge in violence.

Ultra-orthodox spokesmen blamed both the major parties for the violence that marred the election campaign. They drew attention to the central role that comedians played in their television advertisements, and contended that it was symptomatic of the campaign as a whole. Faced with this emptiness, there are those who 'seek satisfaction in other ways'. Their resort to violence is simply a forlorn attempt to fill the vacuum left by the nation's leaders.

The Haredi press also drew attention to the essentially negative nature of the campaign. Both the Likud and the Alignment concentrated their efforts on denigrating their opponents rather than on presenting their own accomplishments and plans for the future. This approach, ultra-orthodox spokesmen insisted, invariably led to verbal violence between the leaders of the two major parties and, in turn, to the physical violence of their more rabid followers.[42]

Even though they made frequent references to these and other aspects of the election campaign, Haredi leaders insisted that the main cause of the upsurge in violence lay elsewhere. The founding fathers had hoped that the Jewish state would be free of crime and violence. Within a short time, however, Israel had not only become as bad as older countries in this respect, it had also become desensitized to the problem, hence the lack of concern about the rising tide of violence and the ever-increasing number of murders. Even the public outcry after the killing of Emil Greenzweig, ultra-orthodox spokesmen insisted, was not motivated by moral considerations. Each side was simply trying to make political capital out of the tragic event.

Paradoxically, however, the causes of the killing were not political. In Haredi eyes, the grenade attack and the earlier election violence were both the direct result of the secularization of Israeli society. To quote Shlomo Lorenz, the head of the Agudat Israel faction in the Knesset:

> For thousands of years religious education provided Jews with complete immunity. None of them transgressed or came near to transgressing the commandment Thou shall not kill. Much to our regret we now see the consequences, in this and other very serious cases, of the fact that education is no longer based on the Torah. Murder has become an everyday event in the Jewish state.[43]

The ultra-orthodox press borrowed a number of images from the natural sciences to emphasize the inevitability of this decline to crime and violence. Two of them – the medical analogy[44] and the organic metaphor[45] – also appeared in the secular media. However, the third one – a vacuum image – was only found in the Haredi press. Political and rabbinical leaders alike used this particular metaphor to emphasize the spiritual emptiness of secular Zionism and explain its deleterious effect on the Jewish state. Society, like nature, they argued, cannot tolerate a vacuum. Negative phenomena like crime and violence therefore come to fill the void created by the rejection of Judaism. In the oft-quoted aphorism of the Book of Proverbs (29:18), Where there is no vision, the people cast off restraint.

The process of secularization was sometimes portrayed as a kind of cultural diffusion. Israelis had simply adopted certain behavioural patterns from abroad, especially from the United States. More commonly though, it was conceived of as a kind of purposive action on the part of the founding fathers. They had done their utmost to subvert Jewish tradition, especially among the new immigrants of North African and Asian origin who arrived in Israel during the mass *aliya* of the 1950s. However, the leaders of the nascent Jewish state had failed to take certain inexorable trends into account. They did not realize that for those who go beyond the four cubits of Jewish law 'there are no limits and anything goes'.

Haredi politicians, in common with some of their secular counterparts, called for a much more determined response on the part of both the police and the judiciary. However, they were also at pains to point out the limitations of this law-and-order approach since the upsurge of political and other forms of violence was due to 'the bankruptcy of secularism'. Only 'a spiritual revolution and a return to the Torah' could prevent a worsening of the situation. There is simply no other way of dealing with the problem.

ETIOLOGY STORIES[46]

The condemnation of the attacks on Alignment property and persons and the grenade attack on the Peace Now demonstration did not focus on those who actually carried them out. It concentrated instead on the words and deeds of those who allegedly encouraged them. Critics of the government differed as to whether the violence on the streets was an intended or unintended consequence of verbal violence. Without exception, however, they took Begin, Sharon and the other Likud leaders to task for their denial of the victims. By denigrating those who disagreed with the government as traitors or saboteurs, they turned them into legitimate targets in the eyes of their more volatile supporters.

Although the Likud leaders completely rejected the opposition's etiology stories about the violence on the streets they could not remain oblivious to them. They had to offer alternative ones. Thus, besides placing the issue of violence on the public agenda, the Alignment and its extra-parliamentary allies also set the parameters of the debate about the problem. The controversy centred not on the perpetrators of the violence but on their alleged auxiliaries. Everyone was concerned with the question as to who was causally and politically responsible for the violence.

Reviewing the etiology and counter-etiology stories about the violence that occurred during the election campaign and at the Peace Now demonstration draws attention to the way in which they differ from those concerning other instances of street violence in Israel. Previous studies have shown how violent demonstrations of both Arabs and Jews were attributed to the influence of 'extremist' leaders at both ends of the political spectrum.[47] Using the corrupter–corrupted model, protagonists of all persuasions emphasized the rhetoric of the few to depoliticize the actions of the many. However, in the cases under investigation exactly the opposite happened. The behaviour of demonstrators on the streets was used to stigmatize those in the corridors of power. The corrupted provided the grounds for the delegitimization of the corrupters rather than the other way round.

Clearly, these two applications of the corrupter–corrupted model have very different consequences for the society in which they occur. Whereas the delegitimation of the corrupted leads to a more or less united front against the perpetrators of violence, the delegitimation of the corrupters causes a deepening of divisions within the body politic. While the former generates widespread consensus throughout the society in question, the latter sharpens the conflict between its constituent parts.

But this use of the corrupter–corrupted model is, of course, not only the cause of the divisions within Israeli society, it is also the result of them. The contours of the debate as to who was causally responsible for the violence on the streets mirrors the cleavages between the different camps – right and left, religious and secular – that have characterized the Israeli body politic ever since the establishment of the state, and especially since the Likud took over the reins of power in 1977. As Sidney Verba wrote in the aftermath of the assassination of President Kennedy, crises can have a major integrative or disintegrative effect, but they usually reinforce the tendency that is strongest in the society in question.[48]

NOTES

1. As such it constitutes a classic example of the 'important neglected paradox' that elections lead to violence. For a pioneering analysis of this phenomenon see David C. Rapoport and Leonard Weinberg, 'Elections and Violence', *Terrorism and Political Violence* 12/3 and 4 (Autumn/Winter 2000), pp. 15–50.
2. Shimon Peres recently revealed that on several occasions during the election campaign the Israeli Police and Israeli Secret Service warned of plans to assassinate him.
3. *Yediot Achronot*, 14 February 1983.
4. Yona Avrushmi was subsequently found guilty of the murder of Emil Greenzweig and the attempted murder of nine other demonstrators. He was sentenced to life imprisonment.
5. Moshe Shahal, the chairman of the Alignment faction in the Knesset, introduced a private member's bill that proposed punishing political parties whose supporters engaged in violence. Commenting on the idea, one political columnist drew attention to the fact that a similar arrangement exists for soccer clubs whose fans go on the rampage.
6. *Davar*, 16 June 1981.
7. *Ha'aretz*, 27 February 1983.
8. *Davar*, 17 June 1981.
9. Other Likud leaders were criticized for referring to their party and its coalition partners as the national camp, thereby implying that the Alignment and its allies were less patriotic and Zionist than them.

10. Although all the opposition leaders were agreed as to the deleterious consequences of this kind of incitement, there were those who objected to the use of the expression 'verbal violence'. Some simply pointed out that it was a contradiction in terms. Others expressed concern that it could lead to undesirable restrictions on the freedom of speech, and therefore urged the use of a more precise legal concept such as incitement to murder.
11. *Davar*, 11 February 1983.
12. Ibid.
13. This term is derived from the acronym of the Hebrew name of the PLO and is used to refer in a pejorative way to Jews who are considered to be overly sympathetic to the Arab cause.
14. The attacks on the 'leftist mafia' that allegedly controlled the Israeli television were also regarded as an attempt to 'delegitimate the opposition struggle'.
15. *Al Hamishmar*, 11 February 1983.
16. *Ha'aretz*, 16 June 1981.
17. Alignment leaders also claimed that those concerned always apologized for their deprecating remarks, and were publicly reprimanded for having made them. Consequently, their verbal violence had never led to physical attacks on Likud leaders or on their supporters.
18. *Divrei HaKnesset* 96 (1983), p. 1369. Sarid argued that these allegations were particularly wicked because nobody believed them. Those concerned were simply engaged in 'cynical incitement in an attempt to gain votes'.
19. *Al Hamishmar*, 17 June 1981.
20. *Al Hamishmar*, 17 February 1983.
21. This was rather ironic, considering Menachem Begin's constant invocation of the Holocaust as a legitimation of his government's foreign policy in general and his attitude towards Israel's Arab neighbours in particular. On this point see pages 114–18.
22. This term was first coined by Daniel Bar-Tal 'The Monopoly of Patriotism', in Daniel Bar-Tal and Ervin Staub (eds), *Patriotism in the Lives of Individuals and Nations* (Chicago, IL: Nelson Hall, 1977), pp. 246–70.
23. *Ha'aretz*, 14 February 1983.
24. *Divrei HaKnesset* 96 (1983), p. 1372.
25. Yossi Sarid and Yair Tzaban, two Alignment members of the Knesset, made frequent complaints about the lack of police resolve in the investigation of the killing of Emil Greenzweig. When Yona Avrushmi was eventually arrested on suspicion of the murder, they and others claimed that he had been fortuitously discovered by an undercover agent working with drug addicts rather than by the special unit set up to investigate the grenade attack. From 1982 onwards, Yossi Sarid often referred to a report by Yehudit Karp, the deputy Attorney-General, that documented the lack of concerted police and judicial action against Jewish settlers who engaged in violence against a local Arab population.
26. *Divrei HaKnesset* 96 (1983), pp. 1368–9.
27. *Al Hamishmar*, 18 February 1983.
28. Ibid.
29. Politicians and publicists alike resorted to a war analogy to drive this message home. They referred to the streets as 'a new front in our struggle for survival', and described Emil Greenzweig as 'having fallen while fulfilling his duty as a citizen'. In a similar vein, Yehezkel Zakai, an Alignment Member of Knesset introduced a private member's bill to the effect that anybody killed or injured at a demonstration would be entitled to compensation like those who fell or were wounded in battle.
30. *Al Hamishmar*, 11 February 1983.
31. *Davar*, 24 June 1981.
32. There were also those who suggested that it was an Arab rather than a Jew who threw the grenade.
33. Not only did Alignment leaders refuse to admit to any wrongdoing. They cited the fact that Avrushmi was a 'lone wolf' and politically unaffiliated as further evidence of the far-reaching influence of verbal violence on those with a low level of self-restraint.
34. Likud leaders sometimes claimed that the election violence was caused by Alignment agents provocateurs. They also suggested that someone on the Israeli left had thrown the grenade at the 'Peace Now' demonstration in an attempt to embarrass the government.
35. *Ma'ariv*, 28 April 1981.

36. This term was used to compare supporters of the Likud with those of Ayatollah Khomeini.
37. *Nekuda*, 27 February 1983. According to Ha'ezni, Gush Emunim was blamed by the left for the death of Emil Greenzweig, in the same way that it was held responsible for the plight of the slums, the failure to achieve peace and other problems. He contended that the settler movement filled an indispensable role — that of the scapegoat Jew.
38. *Ha'ir*, 18 February 1983.
39. *Ha'aretz*, 23 February 1983.
40. *Divrei Knesset* 96 (1983), p. 1307. The Likud and the Alignment nevertheless found it impossible to submit a joint parliamentary motion concerning the grenade attack because they could not agree about the extent to which each of them was responsible for the incident.
41. This designation is based on a verse in Isaiah (66:5): Hear the word of the Lord, you who tremble [*haredim*] at His word.
42. Avraham Shapiro, a Member of Knesset for Agudat Yisrael took this argument one step further: 'Violence', he claimed, 'does not begin with grenades. It starts with thoughts, continues with words and ends with deeds.'
43. *Hamodia*, 11 February 1983. Haredi political and spiritual leaders attribute not only murder, but every kind of crime and delinquency to secularism. For an analysis of the major contours of this argument see Gerald Cromer, 'Secularism is the Root of All Evil: The Haredi Response to Crime and Delinquency', *International Journal of Group Tensions* 26/2 (Summer 1996), pp. 104–21.
44. Susan Sontag, *Illness as Metaphor* (New York: Vintage Books, 1979).
45. Stuart Hall, Chas Critcher, Tony Jefferson, John Clark and Brian Roberts, *Policing the Crisis: Mugging, the State, and Law and Order* (London: Macmillan, 1978), p. 102.
46. This term is borrowed from Edwin Pfuhl, *The Deviance Process* (New York: D. Van Nostrand, 1980), p. 142.
47. See, for instance, Alina Koren, 'The Coverage of Land Day in the Israeli Press', *Patuach* 2 (Summer 1994), pp. 10–11, and Ada Yurman, 'The Social Reaction to the Wadi Salib Riots 1959' (unpublished MA thesis, Bar Ilan University, Ramat Gan, 1994; in Hebrew), pp. 37–8.
48. Sidney Verba, 'The Kennedy Assassination and the Nature of Political Commitment', in Bradley S. Greenberg and Edwin B. Parker (eds), *The Kennedy Assassination and the American Public: Social Communication in Crisis* (Stanford, CA: Stanford University Press, 1965), p. 357.

6
Racism

THE FINAL BETRAYAL

The elections to the 11th Knesset in July 1984 led to a stalemate between the two major political blocs and, in turn, to the establishment of the National Unity government. Henceforth, the Likud had to share the spoils of office not only with its parliamentary allies but also with the rival Labour Party. Not surprisingly, even this partial changeover of power had a crucial influence on the stigma contests between the opposing camps. The controversy about the war in Lebanon subsided, the debate concerning the past became much more limited in scope, and although the dispute regarding the government's causal responsibility for the violence of non-state actors continued, it did so in a different guise.

The stigma contest surrounding Meir Kahane's election to the Knesset and his subsequent meteoric rise in popularity focused, to a large extent at least, on the causal responsibility of the leaders of the nationalist camp. Even though this particular controversy took place after the period of Likud rule it is included in the present study. An analysis of its major contours provides an additional perspective on the stigma contests covered in the previous chapters, and enables us to extend the implications drawn in the concluding one.

Meir Kahane, the leader of the newly elected Kach Party, rejected the idea that the Israeli body politic had become more polarized while the Likud was in power. In fact, he held that exactly the opposite was the case. The ideological differences between the camps, Kahane insisted, had been obliterated. Menachem Begin and his colleagues had betrayed the ideas of their revered mentor, Ze'ev Jabotinsky, and abandoned his distinctive vision of the Jewish state. Not only did they fail to annex the territories liberated during the Six Day War, they had returned the Sinai Peninsula to Egypt and agreed to grant autonomy to the Palestinians in Gaza and on the West Bank. There was, therefore, no difference between the two major parties. 'One was shameful, the other a disgrace.'

According to Kahane, the situation was worsened by the fact that those to the right of the Likud were essentially the same. Both the more hawkish political parties and the extra-parliamentary settlers' movements only differed on minor issues such as the number of settlements to be built over the Green Line. None of them was prepared to take the radical steps necessary to ensure the physical and spiritual survival of the Jewish state. Only he, Kahane, remained loyal to the principles that the national camp was meant to represent.[1]

This view of the Israeli body politic is, of course, a mirror image of the reaction that Kahane himself is thought to have engendered on being elected to the Knesset. However, the response was much more complicated than many observers would have us believe. Although, as Aviezer Ravitsky has pointed out, Kahane was 'roundly condemned by spokesmen representing the entire ideological and political spectrum'[2] he was by no means regarded as *sui generis*. Protagonists of all persuasions tried to point out the similarity and/or the interaction between him and their ideological rivals. They were simultaneously involved in a struggle against a common foe and in conflict with each other.

THEY MUST GO

Kahane initially contended that 'going home' to Israel was the only viable solution to the problem of intermarriage in the diaspora. Only there, he argued, can Jews 'preserve and create their own specific tradition and way of life, free of the spiritual and social assimilation of a foreign and abrasive culture'.[3] Subsequently, Kahane took a much less sanguine view of the situation. Israel, he bemoaned, is as devoid of Jewish content as the diaspora and is, therefore, also hit by the plague of intermarriage. To counter the situation, Kahane tabled a private bill 'for the prevention of assimilation between Jews and non-Jews and the holiness of the People of Israel'. According to the provisions of this proposed law, separate educational institutions and public beaches would be created, non-Jews would be prevented from residing in Jewish neighbourhoods except with the majority consent of the Jewish dwellers, and it would be forbidden for Jewish citizens and residents of the state to marry or have sexual relations with non-Jews.[4]

But it is not only marriage to gentiles that constitutes a threat to the survival of the Jewish state. According to Kahane, their mere presence in the country does so. Israel, he argued, is endangered above all by the exceptionally high birth-rate among Arabs on both sides of the Green Line. This, together with a number of demographic trends amongst Israeli Jews (for example, a much lower birth-rate, a large number of abortions, the continuing decline in immigration, and steady increase in emigration), constitutes a threat to the minimal conception of Zionism – a state with a Jewish majority. If these trends were not reversed, the Arabs would sooner or later be able to 'peacefully, quietly and nonviolently become the majority in Israel, and then democratically vote the Jewish state out of existence'.[5] Kahane put forward a number of ideas as to how this threat should be dealt with. All of them, however, were designed to achieve two goals – a reduction in the number of Arabs living in Israel and the 'political neutralization' of those who remained.

The first of these proposals called for the establishment of an Emigration Fund for Peace, which would be used to provide Arabs with financial inducements to leave the country, and tax exemptions for all residents of the territories conquered in 1967 who opted for non-citizenship. Both ideas, however, became increasingly radical and culminated in Kahane's private member's bill concerning 'Israeli citizenship and a population transfer between Jews and Arabs'. The proposed law advocated the restriction of citizenship to members of the Jewish people. Non-Jews wishing to live in Israel would only be able to do so as 'resident strangers', without the right to be elected to public office or to vote in the elections to the Knesset and other public institutions. Those who were not prepared to accept this status would have the option of leaving the country willingly and receiving compensation for their property, or being forcibly removed.[6]

According to Kahane, these bills were the only way of dealing effectively with the twin threats, spiritual and physical, to the continued existence of the State of Israel. Any Jew with 'a modicum of an instinct of self-preservation' should therefore support them. However, this pragmatic argument was by no means the only or even the main one that Kahane cited in favour of the proposed laws. He also defended them on halachic grounds – as the 'embodiment of Jewish law' concerning marriage to gentiles and the conditions under which they are allowed to remain in the Holy Land – and as a necessary prerequisite for the final redemption.

Kahane believed that the Messiah would come only when the degradation of the Jews and the consequent Hillul Hashem – desecration of God's name – were brought to an end. Sexual relationships with non-Jews therefore had to be outlawed, because they 'defile the seed of the Holy People, and strike at the God of Israel through the daughters of His people'.[7] Even more importantly, the Arabs must be evicted from the Land of Israel because their very presence constitutes a desecration of God's name. Their transfer, Kahane insisted, becomes

> more than a political issue. *It is a religious issue, a religious obligation, a commandment to erase Hillul Hashem.* Far from fearing what the Gentiles will do if we do such a thing, let the Jew tremble as he considers the anger of the Almighty *if we do not*. The great redemption can come immediately and magnificently if we do that which God demands. One of the great yardsticks of *real* Jewish faith in this time of momentous decisions is our willingness to reject fear of man in favour of awe of God, and remove the Arabs from Israel ... Let us remove the Arabs from Israel and bring redemption. *They must go.*[8]

But Kahane was pessimistic as to the chances of this happening. He felt that the Jews were unable to take this leap of faith. Their belief, not only in God but also in themselves, had been destroyed by the 'Arabs within'.

HEIL KAHANE

Politicians of all persuasions drew attention to the negative aspects of Meir Kahane's biography and personality. There were constant references to his tempestuous love affairs and contacts with the Mafia, and repeated assertions that he was fuelled by an insatiable drive for publicity. Kahane's detractors claimed he was 'a person full of deep contradictions and strong impulses, with a highly dubious biography'.[9]

Kahane's supporters were attacked on similar grounds. Yair Kotler's portrayal of the Kach constituency is typical of this kind of onslaught. He argued that Kahane was,

> left with those on the fringe of society: teenagers from broken homes, drug addicts, *ba'alei teshuvah* – Jews who have abandoned their former

lifestyles and returned to Orthodox Judaism, residents of deteriorating neighbourhoods in the United States and of development towns in Israel, the unemployed, Arab haters, and the unbalanced, looking for action.[10]

This personal discreditation was accompanied by an ideational critique. Meir Kahane's entry into the Knesset prompted a frontal attack on his policies and the ideology on which they were based. His racism, it was argued, placed him beyond the pale. To quote Noah Moses, the editor of *Yediot Achronot*, Israel's most widely read newspaper:

> In the same way as the PLO is outside the consensus because of its racist stance, which does not recognize the basic right of the Jews to live in the Land of Israel, so the racism of Kahane is outside the consensus because it does not recognize the right of the Arabs to do so. Kahane is beyond the borders of Zionism, because Zionism and racism are contradictory concepts. Kahane is not just another, more extreme, national movement. There is a red line between Herut, Techiya and Kahane ... In the struggle against racism we stand together, Left and Right, from Mapam to Techiya. Only the unified opposition of the Zionist public can outlaw racism, place it beyond the pale, and draw the border which must under no circumstances be crossed.[11]

But those who placed Kahane beyond the pale, or over the red line, not only did so on the grounds that he was outside the Zionist consensus, they claimed that his worldview was opposed to 'all the values, both Western and Jewish, that are dear to us'. Thus, President Herzog explained his refusal to invite a representative of the Kach Party to consultations on the formation of a government, in terms of Kahane's 'abrogation of civil rights and his negation of the principles of the Torah of Israel'.[12] In a similar vein, Yitzhak Zamir, the Attorney General, attacked Kahanism on the grounds that it 'contradicts the principle of international law and the standards of civilized nations', and 'distorts Judaism by presenting a biased picture of the tradition and heritage of the Jewish people'.[13]

Holocaust survivors and others argued that, pernicious as Kahanism was, it must not, indeed cannot, be compared with Nazism. Aharon Megged for instance, emphasized the need to remember the 'small difference' between them. 'The honorary title Nazi cannot be distributed lavishly', he insisted, because it is 'unique, and refers to a very particular kind of satanic behaviour'.[14] But protestations of this nature were of little or no avail. Comparisons were constantly made between Kahane's worldview and that of Nazi Germany. He himself was often portrayed as a kind of modern-day *führer*. One biography, for instance, bears the title Heil Kahane! His supporters were compared to the Hitler Youth. The only difference between them was the colour of their shirts – yellow instead of brown. And most importantly, Kahane's ideology was depicted as 'a Jewish variation of Nazism', or 'a *Judenrein* in reverse'.

This particular comparison was most clearly expressed in Michael Eitan's speech to the Knesset House Committee, in favour of limiting Kahane's parliamentary immunity. He drew attention to the striking resemblance between Kahane's private member's bill 'for the prevention of the assimilation between Jews and non-Jews' and the infamous Nuremberg Laws of 1935.[15] The main points of his speech were subsequently reported in tabular form in the afternoon daily *Hadashot* (see table opposite).[16]

Invidious comparisons of this nature were often employed to try and convince political leaders and the general public of the need to take concerted action against Kahane and his supporters. In many instances they were reinforced by analyses of the similarities between the political situation in Israel and that of Weimar Germany (for example, galloping inflation, a failed war), and the failure to take effective action against the Nazis during the early stages of their rise to power. To quote Gideon Hausner, the former Attorney General and government prosecutor at the Eichmann trial: 'We have long accused the Germans of silence in the face of evil. We, of all people, must speak out. Each of us. If we do not, it will be a grave mistake.'[17]

These specific references to the Holocaust were backed up by more general ones to the lessons of Jewish history and traditional Jewish teachings concerning the dignity of man who is created in the image of God. Frequent mention was also made of the concept of a defensive democracy. Thus, in response to the very small number of people who objected to any limitations being placed on Kahane's freedom of speech, the proponents of restrictive measures argued that, 'just as a man need not agree to being killed, so the state need not agree to being eradicated and erased from the map'.[18] When in danger the state can, indeed must, defend itself against its enemies.

These arguments provided the philosophical underpinning for a series of measures designed to prevent the dissemination of Kahane's ideas. A detailed analysis of these administrative and legal reforms is beyond the confines of this study.[19] It is important, however, to mention

Subject	Kahane's Bill	Nazi Legislation
Residential restrictions	Non-Jews may not live within the city limits.	Apartments in Berlin and Munich rented to Jews may not be rented again to the Jew, his wife, or a Jewish undertaking without a special permit.
Prohibition of intermarriage	Male and female Jews, citizens and residents of the state, are forbidden to marry non-Jews both in and out of the country. Mixed marriages will not be recognized.	Marriage between Jews and citizens of German blood is forbidden. Marriages in violation of the law are invalid even if performed outside the country.
Separation of students	All educational institutions in Israel will be segregated between Jews and non-Jews.	It is forbidden for Jewish students to study in German schools. They are only allowed to study in Jewish ones.
Extra-marital relations	A. It is forbidden for male and female Jews who are citizens of the state to have full or partial sexual relations of any kind with non-Jews, including outside marriage. Violation of this provision is to be punished by two years' imprisonment. B. A non-Jew who has sexual relations with a Jewish prostitute or a Jewish male is to be punished by fifty years in prison. A Jewish prostitute or Jewish male who has sexual relations with a non-Jewish male is to be punished by five years in prison.	A. Extra-marital relations between Jews and subjects of the state of German blood or of related blood are forbidden. B. Jews are not permitted to employ in their households subjects of the state of Germany or related blood who are under the age of forty-five.
Prevention of meetings among youth	All summer camps, community centres, and other mixed institutions will be closed. Visits by Jewish and Arab students in villages and homes, overseas trips in which Jewish students are guests in non-Jewish homes, and similar visits by non-Jews in Israel will be discontinued.	It is forbidden to include non-Aryan students in visits to youth hostels. It is intolerable that Jewish students take part in school events in which they may come into contact with Aryan students.

the two major laws that were passed in response to Kahane's entry into the Knesset.

According to the existing law the Central Elections Committee could only bar a party on procedural grounds and not on the basis of its political platform. However, in July 1985, the Knesset passed an amendment to the Basic Law according to which a party could not participate in elections if it incited to racism.[20] This enabled the committee to disqualify Kach in the 1988 elections and to bring Meir Kahane's parliamentary career to an abrupt, and for many, a welcome end.

It had long been an offence to promote feelings of ill-will and enmity between different sections of the population and to publish material that may bring a person into disrepute because of his origin or religion.[21] However, the legislation was never used before Kahane's electoral success and few politicians suggested that it be implemented after his entry into the Knesset. They placed emphasis on the need to enact a new law dealing specifically with the problem of racial incitement. Only in this way, it was argued, would the severity of the offence be made clear to all. After a lengthy and often acrimonious debate the Knesset amended the Penal Law. The new enactment included the following two provisions:

144B. (a) A person who publishes anything with the purpose of stirring up racism is liable to imprisonment for five years.
(b) For the purpose of this section, it shall be immaterial whether or not the publication leads to racism and whether or not it is true.
144D. A person who has in his possession, for distribution, a publication prohibited by section 144B, with a view to stirring up racism, is liable to imprisonment of one year, and the publication shall be forfeited.[22]

Nobody has yet been indicted under the new law, and many legal experts believe that it is highly unlikely that anybody will be in the future. The need for direct proof of *mens rea*, or what is called specific intent, makes it almost impossible to secure a prosecution. The Knesset, they argue, may have to follow the British experience and dispense with this particular condition if the law is to fulfil an instrumental as well as a symbolic function.

THE LONG JOURNEY TO THE RIGHT

As the representative of all sectors of Israeli society, President Herzog portrayed Meir Kahane as an alien intrusion into the national body politic. He was not 'an Israeli creation at all, but a foreign import from the United States'.[23] Leaders of the different political parties, however, adopted a much more partisan stance. They all tried to distance themselves from Kahane and to emphasize his proximity to their ideological rivals.

Hamodia for instance, the official organ of the ultra-orthodox Agudat Yisrael, insisted that Kahane was 'the complete antithesis of Haredi Judaism which is anti-Zionist and opposes the national idea'. He is, in contrast, essentially similar to secular Zionists on both the right and left of the political spectrum. 'The moribund debate between them is not concerned with basic principles; it is merely about style and mode of expression.' They all believe in 'taking our future into our own hands' rather than waiting for the Messiah to come and redeem us.[24]

Yossi Sarid, who moved from Labour to the more dovish Citizens' Rights Movement after the establishment of the National Unity Government argued that:

> Meir Kahane was born on 5 June 1967 ... Whoever wants occupation and does not want separation will get Meir Kahane. Both the Likud which cannot swallow him up by annexation, and the Labour Party which cannot throw him up with territorial compromise, will get Kahane. Now after a generation of occupation he is eating us up, and within the next generation he will consume us ... He was born in June 1967, and his days are the days of the occupation. One thousand symposia will not kill Kahane. Only he who kills the occupation will take the soul out of Kahane and Kahane out of his soul.[25]

Labour spokesmen did not feel the need to answer this kind of allegation. They concentrated their attention instead on attacking the leaders of the national camp. Shimon Peres and his colleagues argued that the sole difference between them and Meir Kahane was that he said openly what they were only prepared to talk about behind closed doors. Frequent reference was made to Menachem Begin's description of Palestinian terrorists as 'two-legged animals' and Rafael Eitan's description of the Arabs in the occupied territories as 'drugged cockroaches in a battle'. These statements, it was argued, revealed the Israeli Right in its true colours – 'as a gallery of Kahanes, of varying but converging views'.[26]

The perceived failure of right-wing politicians, especially religious ones, to censure Kahane was also regarded as a sign of their basic agreement with, or at least their ambivalence towards his political goals and the means he used to achieve them. Thus, the Chief Rabbinate's 'very weak statement' about the need for harmonious relations with the Arab minority, the NRP's opposition to laws forbidding incitement to racism, and the refusal of the religious school system to adopt programmes designed to foster Arab–Jewish coexistence, were all interpreted as a seal of approval or, to quote a *Jerusalem Post* editorial 'a certificate of Kashrut' for Kahane's particular brand of 'clerical fascism'.[27]

Proponents of this point of view not only related to the response or, to be more precise, lack of response to Meir Kahane since he was elected to the Knesset; they also drew attention to the different ways in which the Israeli right had facilitated it in the first place. Politicians and political scientists insisted that it was the logical conclusion of seven years of Likud rule, and the accompanying 'long journey to the right in Israeli society'.

The growing ascendancy of the right-wing factions within the existing parties (for example, the Likud and the NRP) and the establishment of new ones dedicated solely to the idea of a Greater Israel (such as Techiya and Morasha in the 1981 and 1984 Knesset elections, respectively), were regarded as important manifestations of this trend. So, too, was the drift toward 'dangerous violence' – from the vigilante activities against Arabs in the occupied territories, to engaging in civil disobedience against the evacuation of Yamit, and the involvement in terrorist activities in the West Bank – within Gush Emunim. According to many observers the detrimental effects of this trend were heightened by the failure of the law-enforcement authorities to take determined action against those concerned. It created the feeling among the settlers that they were above the law and that the government was on their side.

Immediately after Kahane's entry into the Knesset, Danny Rubinstein, the Arab affairs correspondent for *Davar*, warned that leaders of the national camp would once again fail to take effective action. 'Anybody who believes in and insists upon permanent Israeli sovereignty over the West Bank and Gaza', he argued, knows that solutions such as autonomy and minority rights really have no chance of succeeding. It is, therefore, necessary to deal with the Arabs in another way, and to try and get rid of them. Thus, the leaders of the national camp can be angry about Kahane's style and his violent behaviour, but no more than that ... Kahane is a rather wild but legitimate child of the national camp.[28]

Many observers took this argument a step further. They claimed that Kahane's electoral success was not only the continuation of a long-term trend towards the right but that it also prompted others to move in that direction. Thus, Professor Avishai Margalit, a prominent activist in Peace Now, contended that,

> There are now two approaches in Gush Emunim – one advocating settlement and the other advocating expulsion ... The latter is intent on creating a public atmosphere and public pressure that will lead to the expulsion of the Arabs ... That is the logic behind the demand to completely outlaw the throwing of stones. The only way to achieve this aim is to ensure that there are no Arab children in the West Bank or, in short, to expel all the Arabs ... Kahane himself is on the fringe of Israeli society ... Rabbi Levinger and Daniella Weiss are not on the margin even though they are, to all intents and purposes, Kahanists. Consequently, that rogue is benefiting from their lawlessness, and his work is being done by others.[29]

This process of radicalization, or what Yehoshafat Harkabi aptly referred to as Kahanization,[30] was also apparent among party politicians. In fact, two members of the government (Michael Dekel, the Likud Minister of Agriculture and Yosef Shapira, the NRP Minister Without Portfolio) came out in favour of some kind of programme for the transfer of the Arab population. Sometimes, this trend was explained in terms of the exigencies of electoral politics. After all, public opinion polls indicated a substantial increase in support for the Kach Party, and particularly for its policy toward the Arab minority in Israel.[31] More frequently, however, it was attributed to the fact that Kahane's entry into the Knesset had 'broken the barrier of shame', and given a certain degree of legitimacy to his policies and the ideology on which they were based. Consequently, those who had been wary about expressing such ideas in public now felt free to do so. In particular, advocates of transfer could come out of the closet.

The establishment of the Moledet Party just before the 1988 elections was regarded as the clearest sign of the growing radicalization of the Israeli right. Although it came out in favour of 'voluntary transfer' its leader, Rechavam Ze'evi was not excommunicated or treated as a political outcast. In fact, after protracted negotiations he was appointed Minister Without Portfolio in the Likud government. With this step, many observers considered that the prophecies of doom made immediately after Kahane's entry into the Knesset six years earlier had come true. Just one month after the 1984 elections, the satirist B. Michael had written:

> Kahane's strength is to be found in his lack of shame, in the legitimacy that he gives to other dark forces, in the breaches that he makes in the red line ... Kahane is the AIDS virus in the weary body of Israeli society ... He undermines what remains of its immune system. We will not die from Kahane himself, but he makes it much easier for the fatal illness to develop.[32]

With Ze'evi's appointment to a ministerial post, it seemed to many that the virus had spread to the most central organs of the body politic.

A FALSE PROPHET

Leaders of the Israeli right did not relate to the accusation that they had followed in Meir Kahane's footsteps. They only responded to the allegations regarding their role in having 'prepared the ground' for his electoral success. For reasons that are not readily apparent, spokesmen of the religious Zionist parties were more prone to defend themselves against these charges and to attack those who made them, than their secular counterparts.

Political and spiritual leaders alike attacked what they felt was the sensationalist coverage of Kahane's election to the Knesset. They attributed it to a general tendency to 'cultivate the deviant', and a more specific desire on the part of the Israeli left to use his electoral success for 'anti-nationalist, anti-Land of Israel, anti-religious propaganda'. According to *Hatzofe*, the official organ of the NRP,

> instead of decrying just Kahane, they exploit the whole phenomenon in their unrelenting war against anyone who is contaminated with a little

love of the Land of Israel, and who believes in the religious and historical rights of the Jewish people to the Promised Land.[33]

Spokesmen of the national religious camp made a constant effort to point out that Meir Kahane represented neither religious Zionists nor religious Zionism. Time and again they insisted that only a very small proportion of his supporters came from their ranks. Even more importantly, Kahane's views were not the 'authentic Jewish idea' as he claimed them to be. In fact, exactly the opposite was the case. Political and spiritual leaders alike engaged in a 'war of verses' to show that 'the ways of the Torah are the ways of pleasantness, and all its paths are peace'. Kahane, in contrast, was consistently aggressive. From his first political appearance he had adopted 'the style of the clenched fist'.[34]

This defence of religious Zionism went hand-in-hand with an attack on its detractors. It was the secular left rather than the religious right, settlement leaders insisted, who had paved the way for Kahane's entry into the Knesset. According to this view of things, those who had voted Kach had not done so because they agreed or identified with his worldview, they had simply wished to register a protest against government complacency toward, and leftist sympathy for, Arab trouble-makers.[35] To quote an editorial from *Nekuda*, the journal of the Council of Jewish Settlements in Judea, Samaria and Gaza:

> Most of those among us, and they are relatively few, who voted Kach, did so in response to what appeared to them to be the government's failure to enforce the law against Arab troublemakers, especially those on the roads of Judea and Samaria ... There is no doubt that those who voted Kach did so as a response to the attitudes of Yossi Sarid, Shulamit Aloni and others like them, who ridicule any patriotic Jewish stance, and justify the Arab viewpoint in a sick and anti-nationalist way.[36]

Extremism, in short, begets extremism, and those in the centre, the settlers added, are the ones who suffer the most. After all, Kahane's increasing popularity indicated a growing disbelief in the possibility of Arab–Jewish coexistence and, therefore, in the wisdom of building new settlements in Judea, Samaria and Gaza. This argument had, it seems, turned full circle. Those allegedly responsible for Kahane's electoral success are, according to this way of thinking, its major victims.

While the religious right provided the most vociferous defence of the national camp, it also included a number of rather cogent and fierce critics. Some emphasized the detrimental effects of political infighting and the consequent lack of strong leadership. Kahane, they argued, had come to fill the vacuum. Others blamed 'the stampede to Kahane' on the religious education system. They argued that the schools and the B'nei Akiva youth movement had inculcated 'a one-dimensional, black-and-white view' of the Arab–Israeli conflict. The younger generation was now 'escaping to the extreme' because they were fearful of the extent and intricacy of the problems involved. Only a change in educational priorities could reverse this trend. The current emphasis on simplicity and submission to authority had to be replaced by curricula designed to help the young deal with the complexities of Israeli society, and to assume personal responsibility for it.[37] If Kahane's entry into the Knesset was to prompt this kind of response, his religious critics argued, it could even prove to be a blessing in disguise.

UNFORESEEN CONSEQUENCES

At the height of the public furore following the 1984 elections, one observer, not surprisingly a sociologist, came out 'in favour of Kahane in the Knesset'. The presentation of his ideas in an 'open and institutionalized forum' would, he hoped, force political leaders, especially those of the national camp, to deal with the issues they raised. The time had come for them to 'put their cards on the table' and take a definite stance for or against Kahane's policies and the ideology on which they were based.[38]

According to many observers, the professor's hopes were, in fact, realized. Despite the repolarization that characterized the period of Likud rule, the rival camps came together after the elections to place Kahane beyond the pale. They passed a series of measures to prevent him from disseminating his ideas, and adopted a number of programmes designed to promote alternative ones such as civil rights, democracy and the rule of law. However, this was by no means the whole picture. As Kimmerling and other sociologists know only too well, there are always unforeseen consequences. In this particular case they related to Kahane himself and to his alleged ideological allies.

In accordance with what one journalist aptly referred to as 'the law of relativity' the statements of other right-wing leaders began to sound like the apogee of moderation in comparison with Kahane's vitriolic speeches from the podium of the Knesset.[39] This was reinforced by the fact that the struggle against racial incitement focused almost entirely on Meir Kahane. Even though the legal and educational measures were not conceived of as being *ad hominem*, little or no attention was paid to anyone else besides him. Others continued to disseminate their ideas unabated.

This was particularly surprising since protagonists of all persuasions did not just make a dichotomy between Meir Kahane and the rest of the body politic. Many of them also drew attention to what they felt was an ideological proximity between him and their ideological rivals. This was particularly so in the case of the Israeli left. Politicians and publicists alike were at pains to point out how their right-wing counterparts had not only paved the way for greater acceptance of Kahane's ideas, but had also followed in his footsteps and adopted them.

The first part of this etiology story is, of course, based on the idea of causal responsibility. Had the leaders of the Israeli left continued this line of thought they would have taken Kahane to task for precipitating the post-election radicalization of the national camp. But Shimon Peres and his colleagues did not do so. Once again, they concentrated their attention on other right-wing politicians. At both stages of the etiology story it was the leaders of the national camp who bore the brunt of the attack. First they were inveighed against as facilitators of Kahane's entry into the Knesset, and later for having become his fellow travellers.

Those who made these claims did not, of course, intend to detract in any way from their critique of Kahane himself. They were simply trying to extend the attack to their ideological opponents. However, it may well have had that effect. Emphasizing the similarities and interaction between Kahane and other political leaders makes it more difficult to draw the line between them. If they differ in degree rather than kind, then Kahane can no longer be regarded as evil incarnate. He is just a little worse than others.

NOTES

1. This idea found its clearest expression in the following quotation from a Kach election pamphlet:

   Dear Jew, consider a 100-metre race in which there are three runners. One of them runs 30 metres and falls. The second runs 50 metres and falls. The third runs 90 metres and falls. Who won? None of them. They all lost because in order to win you have to reach the finishing line. The winner is the one who achieves his aim; the one who was prepared to go all the way from the very beginning. Consequently, there is, in the final analysis, no difference between them. Not Shimon Peres, not Yitzhak Shamir, not Ariel and not Geula Cohen ... All of them are part of the silence that will, God forbid, bring upon us a disastrous national calamity.

2. Aviezer Ravitsky, 'Roots of Kahanism: Consciousness and Political Reality', *Jerusalem Quarterly* 39 (1986), pp. 107–8.
3. Meir Kahane, *They Must Go* (New York: Grosset & Dunlop, 1981), p. 55.
4. For an English translation of the bill see Yair Kotler, *Heil Kahane!* (New York: Adama Books, 1986), pp. 198–203.
5. Kahane, *They Must Go*, p. 129. Kahane often portrayed the high Arab birthrate as a kind of political action. He argued that they purposely have a large number of children in order to achieve a majority within the Jewish state.
6. See Kotler, *Heil Kahane!*, pp. 203–8 for an English translation of the bill.
7. Meir Kahane, *Forty Years* (Miami Beach, FL: Institute of the Jewish Idea, 1983), p. 77.
8. Kahane, *They Must Go*, pp. 275–6. Italics in original.
9. Ehud Sprinzak, *Every Man Whatsoever is Right in His Own Eyes: Illegalism in Israeli Society* (Tel Aviv: Sifriat Hapoalim, 1986; in Hebrew), p. 143.
10. Kotler, *Heil Kahane!*, p. 186. Kahane's opponents sometimes adopted exactly the opposite stance, and emphasized the normality of his supporters. Writing about her visit to the Kach Party headquarters in downtown Jerusalem, one correspondent reported that her major surprise was that

> they do not have horns ... The human make-up of Kach constitutes the real revolution that has occurred and the most important signal ... Each one could be your neighbour, your son, or even yourself ... Whoever thinks in terms of lunatics or maniacs is trying to make life easy for himself.

For further details see *Ha'aretz*, 3 August 1984.
11. *Yediot Achronot*, 15 September 1985.
12. This quotation is taken from the presidential statement concerning the decision not to invite a representative of Kach to the consultations on the formation of a government, 1 August 1984.
13. These quotations are taken from the unpublished protocol of the Knesset House Committee's deliberations on the question as to whether Meir Kahane's parliamentary immunity should be restricted.
14. *Davar*, 17 August 1984.
15. Kach subsequently published a similar table comparing 'two murderous covenants' – those of the Nazis and the PLO. For an analysis of the different ways in which Meir Kahane used the Holocaust to legitimate his policies and to delegitimate those of his opponents see Gerald Cromer, 'The Creation of Others: A Case Study of Meir Kahane and His Opponents', in Laurence J. Silberstein and Robert L. Cohn (eds), *The Other in Jewish Thought and History: Constructions of Jewish Culture and Identity* (New York: New York University Press, 1994), pp. 290–2.
16. *Hadashot*, 16 November 1984.
17. *Jerusalem Post*, 3 August 1984.
18. *Hatzaot Hok* 1728, 17 April 1985, p. 194. *Hatzaot Hok* is the official digest of draft parliamentary bills.
19. On this point see Eliezer Lederman and Mala Tabory, 'Criminalization of Racial Incitement in Israel', *Stanford Journal of International Law* 24/1 (Winter 1988), pp. 55–84.
20. Basic Law: The Knesset Amendment No. 9 1155 *Sefer Hahukim* (1985), p. 196. *Sefer Hahukim* is the official digest of Israeli laws. The amendment also disqualified parties that denied either the existence of the State of Israel as the State of the Jewish People or its democratic character.
21. See Lederman and Tabory, 'Criminalization of Racial Incitement', pp. 271–2 for further details of these laws.
22. Penal Law Amendment No. 20 1191 *Sefer Hahukim* (1986), p. 219.
23. *Ha'aretz*, 19 December 1984.
24. *Hamodia*, 10 August 1984.
25. *Ha'aretz*, 4 July 1985.

26. *Jerusalem Post*, 15 August 1988.
27. *Jerusalem Post*, 7 August 1986.
28. *Davar*, 27 July 1984.
29. *Yediot Achronot*, 27 May 1987. Daniella Weiss was the Secretary-General of Gush Emunim from 1985 to 1988. Rabbi Levinger was one of its founders and most influential ideologues. Both were widely regarded as being leaders of the trend toward the extreme right in the settler movement.
30. Yehoshafat Harkabi, *Fateful Decisions* (Tel Aviv: Am Oved, 1986; in Hebrew), p. 231.
31. Kahane received 1.2 per cent of the votes cast for the 11th Knesset in July 1984. By August of the following year public opinion polls predicted that as many as 9 per cent of the electorate would vote Kach.
32. *Hadashot*, 24 August 1984.
33. *Hatzofe*, 2 August 1984. Leaders of the national-religious camp tried to drive this message home by arguing that not a single voice of protest had been raised against the election of two Knesset members from the newly founded Progressive List for Peace, even though it was a 'mouthpiece' for the PLO in Tunis.
34. *Hatzofe*, 26 July 1984.
35. Meir Kahane did, in fact, try to capitalize on this antipathy towards the left. Thus, one of his campaign advertisements read as follows:
    > What will be the response of Yossi Sarid and the Arabs if, God forbid, they hear that Kahane and his views will not be represented in the Knesset. On the other hand, just imagine their faces when they hear that the people have decided to send Rabbi Kahane to the Knesset in order to deal with them. Jews, what message will you send to our enemies? Against Yossi Sarid and his friends – Kahane.
36. *Nekuda*, 8 August 1984. Other national camp spokesmen blamed Kahane's electoral success on the Arabs themselves rather than on their Jewish sympathizers. As far as they were concerned, 'Kahane is just a symptom, and Arab facism is the real demon of the State of Israel.' See, for instance, the columns of Elyakim Ha'ezni, *Hadashot*, 7 July 1984 and Aharon Papu, *Hadashot*, 30 September 1984.
37. *Hatzofe*, 31 October 1984.
38. *Ha'aretz*, 1 August 1984.
39. *Yediot Achronot*, 27 July 1984.

7

Remembering Violence

PAST AND PRESENT

The oft-cited link between nationalism and history is particularly marked in the modern State of Israel. From the very beginning, the future of the Zionist movement was dependent on its ability to create a link with the past. To quote Shmuel Almog:

> The Jews were both more and less of a nation than others. They had age-old traditions yet lacked the most elementary conditions for self-determination. Their Zionism turned towards history to compensate for what was so sorely lacking in the present.[1]

In common with other movements, however, the process of remembering was highly selective. Both the Zionist overview of history and its interpretation of particular events reflected the replacement of religion by nationality as the focus of Jewish identity.

For the Zionist movement the major criterion for evaluating the past was the bond between the Jewish people and their ancient land. It therefore divided history into two major periods – antiquity and exile – and portrayed them in highly positive and negative lights respectively. To bring about a national revival, the Zionist pioneers had to rebel against the oppression and degradation of exile, and recapture the glories of ancient Israel. The creation of a better future involved repudiating the recent past and reviving the golden age that preceded it.

Zionist historiography affected both the degree and nature of the significance attributed to particular events. Hence the marked changes in the importance attached to different Jewish holidays, and the growing emphasis on their political rather than religious significance. In a similar vein, the binary model of Jewish history led to a different understanding of the turning points between the periods. The destruction of the Second Temple ceded pride of place to the Jewish revolts against the Roman Empire at the junction between antiquity and exile, and the Battle of Tel Hai became the symbolic marker for the beginning of the national revival in Palestine. Everything revolved around the struggle for political independence.

With the passage of time, the Holocaust and the newly created State of Israel came to signify the contrast between the fate of Jews in exile and in their own homeland. Zionist leaders contrasted the passivity and persecution of European Jewry with the heroism of those who had struggled for, and gained, independence. Subsequently, however, this dichotomy became much less clear-cut. Politicians of all persuasions began to draw attention to the similarities between Jewish existence in Israel and the diaspora. The Holocaust became a metaphor for a nation that dwells alone, both when scattered among the nations of the world and after returning to its ancient homeland.

But Zionist historiography has not only changed over the years – it has always included several readings of the Jewish past at any particular point in time. The supremacy of the Labour version over those of Revisionist and religious Zionism was both the cause and consequence of its long-standing dominance of the body politic. Not surprisingly therefore, the upheaval had far-reaching effects in this regard. The Likud's assumption of power led to series of disputes about both the distant and recent past. These controversies took different forms, and seemed to focus on different issues. In actual fact, however, they were all concerned in one way or another with a single topic – they all revolved around the subject of violence.

Although these debates were based on differences of opinion about what happened in the past, the question of historical truth was by no means the major bone of contention. The protagonists were primarily concerned with the contemporary situation. Readings of the past were designed to legitimate present actions and policies. That was always the crux of the matter.

THE BAR KOCHBA SYNDROME

In May 1980, less than three years after the Likud-led government assumed the reins of power, Yehoshafat Harkabi, a former head of military intelligence and then professor of international relations at the Hebrew University, called for a national self-reckoning.[2] Fateful decisions had to be made. Fearful that Israeli society was unwilling to tackle the issues head-on, he suggested examining Jewish history. Even though the past does not provide direct analogies to the present, it helps understand the contemporary situation. Nations, like individuals, can, and for that matter should, learn from experience.

Troubled, above all, by the lack of realism of Menachem Begin and his colleagues, Harkabi turned to the Bar Kochba rebellion against the Roman Empire between AD 132 and AD 135, the 'symbol of destructive unrealism' in Jewish history.[3] The revolt, he contended, was doomed to failure from the outset. The Emperor Hadrian had no choice but to crush the rebellion because Palestine constituted a key link in his network of defences. And, as the leader of the only world power with a mighty war machine at his disposal, he had the ability to do so. Although the Jewish forces won a number of impressive victories and even managed to capture Jerusalem for a while, the revolt turned out to be 'the worst disaster in Jewish history'.[4] Not only were more than half of the Jews killed and many others sold into prostitution and slavery within a period of 3 years; the defeat of the Bar Kochba Rebellion signified the beginning of nearly 2,000 years of dispersion.

But for Harkabi the widespread admiration of the revolt – what he referred to as the Bar Kochba Syndrome – was even more disconcerting than the rebellion itself.[5] Rejecting the negative response that characterized Jewish tradition through the ages, many Israelis displayed an unadulterated adulation of the revolt. They glorified Bar Kochba and his fighters regardless of the consequences of their actions. Replacing a morality of responsibility with one of good intentions, Israelis conveniently overlooked the disaster that befell the nation as a result of the rebels' reckless and foolhardy behaviour.

The leaders of the Zionist movement and subsequently of the State of Israel, Harkabi argued, were characterized by a 'practical realistic vision'. They accepted the fact that it is not possible to behave contrary to world opinion. Since the Six Day War, however, and especially after the Likud's rise to power a decade later, the situation had changed dramatically.

> Objective difficulties beset the State of Israel, not the least of which are the intentions of its neighbours ... [but they] have been compounded on the Israeli side by a subjective, psychological and cognitive factor ... [that] stems from an elevation of the myth of unrealism ... Desires and yearnings are accepted as if they were a political programme, and fantasy is enthroned as vision.[6]

According to Harkabi, the myth of unrealism was a major influence on Israeli policy in a wide variety of areas, and particularly with regard to the occupied territories and the war in Lebanon.[7] Political leaders, he insisted, had to accept the fact that 'reality enabled a beginning of the realization of the Zionist dream, but not the complete vision'. They must understand their limitations better than Bar Kochba and his followers did. Otherwise they too will lead the Jewish people to a disaster of monstrous proportions.

Harkabi's views on the revolt and its contemporary implications led to a long and intense debate at a series of public forums and in the columns of the national press. His critics questioned the wisdom of his historical approach in general, and/or the relevance of the Bar Kochba Rebellion to the sovereign State of Israel in particular. However, these misgivings did not prevent them from joining the fray and engaging in exactly the same process. They simply presented a different reading of the past, and suggested alternative solutions to Israel's present predicament.

The revolt, Israel Eldad and others argued, was by no means doomed to failure. Their assessment was based, in part at least, on a more sanguine reading of the situation from a strictly military standpoint. However, this was by no means the only, or even the major reason for their retrospective optimism. Time and again, they emphasized the need to take the spiritual strength of the rebels into account. Their deep commitment to, and willingness to die for, the cause increased their chances of success. Although less tangible than military might, this self-sacrifice was a major component in the balance of forces between the warring sides. Achieving victory over the Roman Empire was, therefore, not as unrealistic as Harkabi would have us believe.[8]

Yigal Yadin, one of the archaeologists who discovered Bar Kochba's letters in the caves of Ein Gedi and a deputy premier in the Likud government, tried to drive this message home by recalling the military experience of the modern Zionist movement. It had faced a series of challenges that were as, or even more awesome than the one that confronted Bar Kochba and his followers. During the early pioneering period, the struggle against the British mandate, the War of Independence, and the wars since the establishment of the state, the Jews faced seemingly insurmountable odds. Nevertheless, they always emerged victorious because of the determination and bravery of those who took up arms against the different enemies. In each case, they showed that any obstacle can be overcome.[9]

Harkabi's critics often took this argument a step further. Victory, they insisted, was not the only criterion by which to judge the rebellion. In the wake of Hadrian's decision to turn Jerusalem into a city of idolatry (Aelia Capitolina) and the imperial decree banning circumcision, Bar Kochba and his followers felt that they had no choice but to take up arms against the Roman Empire. The existing situation was simply unbearable. Like the proverbial proletariat, the rebels had nothing to lose but their chains.

> The greater the duress – and we know duress is not only external, physical, and economic – the less weight is given to the chances of success ... Desperation and belief are the two spiritual forces that override what Harkabi referred to as rational and 'realistic' considerations. Anyone who regards this kind of war as just will not criticize it, whatever the outcome.[10]

Yigal Yadin asked a hypothetical question in order to show the relevance of this argument to the contemporary Israeli situation:

> If, God forbid, the State of Israel wakes up one morning and finds a power like the Soviet Union or its leader issuing a cruel ultimatum, how should it act? ... What will it do if the choice is voluntary liquidation or a devastating war? Will the state spare the lives of its citizens and surrender, or risk their lives, even if the chances of success are very low?[11]

For many of Harkabi's critics this question was, in fact, the crux of the issue. Time and again, they argued that his attack on the Bar Kochba syndrome was just a symptom of a general breakdown in values. The deheroization of the past, Eldad contended, is part of the de-Zionization of Israeli society.[12] Unless this trend is countered, the Jewish state would find itself in dire straits. This internal threat was much more dangerous than any of the external ones facing the country.

Notwithstanding the importance attached to Bar Kochba in Revisionist Zionism, Menachem Begin and his colleagues did not take an active part in the debate. However, the government's decision to arrange an elaborate state reburial of the bones of some of Bar Kochba's followers found 20 years earlier was a clear indication of where it stood on the matter. Despite widespread criticism[13] the Likud-led administration was determined to show their admiration of the rebellion, and to spell out its implications for the Jewish state. Thus, in his eulogy for the reinterred fighters, Menachem Begin reminded the dignitaries gathered in the Judean desert and the television audience at home, that it was the Emperor Hadrian who changed the name of Judea to Palestine, and then went on to declare:

> Our glorious fathers we have a message for you. We have returned to the place whence we came. The people of Israel live and will live in the homeland of Eretz Yisrael [the Land of Israel] for generations upon generations. Glorious fathers we are back, and we will not budge from here.[14]

According to Menachem Begin, the present and future are inextricably intertwined with the past. Bar Kochba and his followers were defeated, but their bravery and courage provided inspiration for the generations to come. We, and therefore they, have emerged victorious. Our glorious forefathers lost the battle, but through their regenerative sacrifice we and they won the war.

THE NEW HEBREW

In May 1920 the settlement of Tel Hai, one of four in the Upper Galilee, was attacked by the neighbouring Arabs. Five settlers were killed in the ensuing battle and the group's commander, Yosef Trumpeldor, was critically wounded and died a few hours later. Those who survived the attack decided to leave for nearby Kfar Giladi. Two days later, upon hearing that a large Arab force was approaching, they withdrew from the French-controlled region and moved south, to the territory under the British mandate.

The battle for Tel Hai provided the state-in-the-making with a myth of origins. The settlers, and Trumpeldor in particular, became the symbol of the New Hebrew, the antithesis of the stereotyped image of the exilic Jew.[15] The leaders of the Yishuv hailed their commitment to build new settlements, and their willingness to sacrifice their lives defending them. The battle was soon marked by an annual remembrance day, and the graves of the fallen became a site of pilgrimage. As national heroes, they were commemorated in both time and space.

Despite, or maybe because of its centrality in the life of the Yishuv, the legend of Tel Hai became a bone of contention between the different strands of Zionism. Each camp tried to appropriate the name Trumpeldor in order to gain legitimacy for its actions and ideology.

Thus, both the pioneer work legions associated with Labour Zionism and the Revisionist youth movement Betar were called after him.[16] However, this nomenculture was just part of a much broader struggle between the rival camps about the legacy of Tel Hai and its revered leader.

Revisionists and socialists alike portrayed Yosef Trumpeldor as the personification of their brand of Zionism. Thus, Jabotinsky and his followers focused entirely on his courage and willingness to sacrifice his life at the altar of the motherland. In their eyes Trumpeldor was the epitome of Zionist monism. Labour leaders, in contrast, drew attention to the way in which Trumpeldor's heroism was accompanied by a deep commitment to settling and working the land. He exemplified their long-standing determination to create a synthesis between nationalism and socialism, and thereby create a just society in the Promised Land.

For reasons related to both the nature of the legend and changes taking place in the society in which it was told, the battle of Tel Hai gradually lost its primacy. In fact, as Yael Zerubavel has pointed out, jokes and parodies about Trumpeldor led to a subversion of the myth and a transgression of its sacredness.[17] Nevertheless, the perceived analogy between the dilemma of Tel Hai and the one surrounding the dismantling of the settlements in the Sinai Peninsula as part of the Camp David accords prompted protagonists of all persuasions to cite events of yesteryear in support of their political and ideological stance.

The debate was sparked off by a series of radio programmes and a book by the journalist Nakdimon Rogel.[18] In a wide-ranging critique of the commemorative narrative about the battle of Tel Hai, he drew attention to the fact that although the settlers had made a firm commitment not to leave, and the leadership of the Yishuv supported an anti-withdrawal policy, they were forced to retreat first from Tel Hai, and subsequently from the northern Galilee as a whole. Even more importantly, Rogel argued, their struggle had no effect whatsoever on the final agreement between the French and the British on the location of the northern border of Palestine. The efforts of Josef Trumpeldor and his fellow-fighters were unsuccessful and, in the final analysis, to no avail.

Rogel's critics saw things very differently. The settlers' heroism, they argued, was worthy of praise and admiration despite their eventual defeat. As such, it made a deep impact on the future military and settlement efforts of the Yishuv. Thus, the replacement of Hashomer (The Watchman) by the more broad-based and voluntaristic Haganah was attributed to the example set by Trumpeldor and his followers. So too were the tower and stockade (*homa umigdal*) settlements established at strategic points around the country at the end of the 1930s. In this regard, the actual events at Tel Hai were irrelevant, it was the myth they gave rise to that mattered, because,

> as always, it was directed to an educational goal, to the setting of an example to the generations to come. It is almost possible to say that the educational aim is to turn the myth of the past into the reality of the future ... because the myth of Tel Hai was the embodiment of the philosophy of settlement and Jewish defence in the Land of Israel throughout the period of the mandate.[19]

There was also a great deal of controversy concerning the lessons to be learnt from the battle of Tel Hai. Protagonists of all persuasions cited Trumpeldor and his fellow fighters in support of their position on the establishment or dismantling of settlements over the Green Line.[20] Gush Emunim, for instance, called on others to act in accordance with Trumpeldor's legacy, and right-wing politicians criticized the Likud government for not doing so. Thus, Zvi Shiloah, the chairman of the Movement for a Greater Israel and a member of Knesset for the Techiya Party, attacked the Prime Minister,

> [for] leading Zionism to a small Israel, or to what Sadat called its natural dimensions not including one grain of holy Arab soil ... to the destruction of the major myth of the last hundred years – that led to the expansion of borders as epitomized in the myth of Tel Hai ... and to the opening of a new era in the history of Zionism – the era of capitulation.[21]

Labour leaders saw things very differently. They recalled the Revisionists' indifference, and even opposition to establishing settlements during the period of the Yishuv, and attacked their support of 'futile' ones in the occupied territories. In their view, the Camp David Accords provided a glimmer of hope in the Arab–Israel conflict:

> The withdrawal from the Sinai Peninsula makes peace with Egypt possible and also the breaking down of the worst psychological barrier that has weighed on Israeli relations with its neighbours – the myth of Zionist expansionism. Zionism was actualized *dunam* after *dunam*. From one tower and stockade settlement to another we achieved

statehood. However, nothing contributed more to the Arab belief that the essence of Zionism is endless expansionism. The withdrawal from the Sinai Peninsula in exchange for real peace is likely to break the chain reaction of war and expansion, expansion and war, and be a stepping stone to a broader peace.[22]

Protagonists of all persuasions were of the opinion that the government's willingness to return the Sinai Peninsula to Egypt signified the demise of the Zionist myth about settling the land. Whether they embraced or rejected this development depended, of course, on whether they were on the right or left of the political spectrum.

NEVER AGAIN

In his speech at the signing of the Israeli–Egyptian peace treaty, Menachem Begin recited Psalm 126 about the return to Jerusalem at the end of the first exile. Before doing so he explained,

> it is the proper place and appropriate time to bring back to memory the song and prayer of thanksgiving I learned as a child in the home of my father and mother. It doesn't exist anymore because they were among the six million people, men, women and children, who sanctified the Lord's name with their sacred blood. The blood which reddened the rivers of Europe from the Rhine to the Danube, from the Bug to the Volga, because they were born Jews, and because they didn't have a country of their own, or a valiant Jewish army to defend them, and because nobody, nobody, came to their rescue, although they cried out, 'Save us! Save us!', *de profundis*, from the depths of the pit and agony.[23]

Even, or maybe especially, on that occasion, the Prime Minister felt the need to relate to the Holocaust. The hope of peace in the future brought to mind the horrors of the past. But this was by no means the only instance in which he did so. Time and again, Menachem Begin referred to the evils of the Nazi period and projected them on to the situation facing contemporary Israel.[24]

Never, since God created man and Satan, the Prime Minister declared, had there been such a wicked and depraved people as those of Nazi Germany. Although opposed to the concept of collective guilt because it had led to so much Jewish suffering, he felt that they were an exception to the rule. Each and every German, Begin insisted, was responsible for the fate of European Jewry. But they were not the only ones to blame. The British government, for instance, had restricted immigration into Palestine and thereby sealed the fate of many Jews. Other countries actively collaborated in, or at least turned a blind eye to the genocide being carried out throughout Europe. They were also guilty. Each and every one of them had to 'account for their behavior in front of God and man'.

Menachem Begin was also wont to make comparisons between the PLO and different aspects of Nazi Germany. The Palestine Covenant, he argued, was *Mein Kampf* No. 2, and the 'organization of murderers' and its leader were the modern-day equivalent of the SS and Adolph Hitler respectively. Thus, in a letter that he sent to President Reagan during the siege of Beirut, Begin wrote: 'I feel as a Prime Minister empowered to instruct a valiant army facing Berlin where, amongst innocent civilians, Hitler and his trenchmen hide in a bunker deep beneath the surface.'[25] The analogy could not be any clearer.[26]

In many instances, Begin drew attention to the fact that the prime enemy of the Jewish people was once again helped, or at least not hindered, by others. He castigated the Soviet Union for providing the PLO with arms and training them how to use them, criticized Western governments for agreeing to the establishment of PLO offices in their countries, and reprehended the United Nations for according the organization observer status. In each case the underlying message was the same – nobody has learnt the lessons of the Holocaust.

Menachem Begin, in contrast, was always willing to spell out the implications of the destruction of European Jewry for the State of Israel. Never again can the Jews allow themselves to be dependent on the good will of others. The task of the postwar generation is to ensure that the Jewish state is able to defend itself against any form of aggression. Thus, in his statement to the Knesset after the PLO attack on the coastal highway, the Prime Minister declared that,

> The days when it was possible to spill Jewish blood and get away with it are over. Under no circumstances will we accept the raising of a hand against a Jewish child or woman. We will do what is incumbent upon us to defend our people. This cruel enemy wants to crush our spirit in order to uproot us from our land. They will not succeed ... We know our goals especially in the generation of the Holocaust and revival. To defend this small people with all the means at our disposal, and to ensure the future of the nation in the Land of Israel.[27]

The Likud-led administration amended the State Education Law in order to give a more central role to the consciousness of the Holocaust and heroism in the national school system, and thereby ensure that this message was transmitted to the younger generation. In addition, Menachem Begin suggested moving the annual Remembrance Day to the ninth of Av when, according to Jewish tradition, both the First and Second Temples were destroyed. Adopting the rabbinic practice of collapsing commemoration[28] Begin argued, was the best way to make sure that the lessons of the Holocaust will be remembered 'for generations'. However, the idea met with vehement opposition from Holocaust survivors and was quickly shelved.

Menachem Begin used analogies between the Nazi period and the contemporary one to justify his government's policy on a wide variety of issues. Its refusal to return territories captured in the Six Day War, for instance, was compared to the continuing Soviet and Polish presence in those regions annexed from Germany after the Second World War. In both instances, Begin argued that the areas in question were captured during the course of a defensive, and therefore just, war. Israel was in no way errant in this respect; it was simply following the example set by others.

The Likud-led administration, in common with earlier Labour ones, adamantly refused to negotiate with the PLO. There was no difference between the two major parties in this regard. However, Menachem Begin and his colleagues invariably justified their long-standing policy in terms of the Holocaust. Thus, the Prime Minister rejected the comparison to the FLN (Front de la Liberation National/National Liberation Front) and the IRA. Their aims were limited to getting the foreign powers out of Algeria and Northern Ireland respectively. The PLO, in contrast, had adopted the genocidal policies of Nazi Germany. They were intent on destroying the Jewish state and driving all its inhabitants into the sea.

This 'banalization of the Holocaust' came under heavy criticism.[29] Time and again, Menachem Begin was accused of drawing 'false' or 'delusionary and dangerous' analogies between the Nazi period and contemporary Israel.[30] Thus, in a parliamentary question about the Prime Minister's reported statement that Israel was faced with the choice between Treblinka and the invasion of Lebanon, an Alignment member of Knesset asked whether he really believed that the PLO was capable of defeating the Israeli army and completely destroying the State of Israel like the Nazis had wiped out the Jews in the death camp.

Or, as one newspaper columnist subsequently put it, 'Beirut is not Berlin.' Arafat's actions, wicked as they may be, cannot be compared to those of Adolph Hitler.[31]

Some of Begin's critics took this argument a step further. In addition to criticizing the Prime Minister for exaggerating the dangers and depravity of the PLO, they accused him of belittling those aspects of Nazi Germany. According to Boaz Evron,

> The Nazi phenomenon was *sui generis*. Under no circumstances should we use terms such as Nazis and SS freely. Doing so makes people forget their initial meaning ... If the PLO is the SS, and the others are Nazis or collaborators with Nazis, people will ask themselves: 'So what was so terrible about the Nazis? It is just a derogatory term used to refer to anyone you don't like.' Consequently, Mr Begin is helping to empty these terms of their original content ... After him it will be impossible to allude to the Holocaust even when it is justifiable to do so. That horse is already dead.[32]

Evron and others did not only oppose Menachem Begin's lessons of the Holocaust, they also pointed to the need to learn an alternative one. The novelist A.B. Yehoshua, for instance, contended that,

> Having experienced in the flesh the price of racism and extreme nationalism we must reject their manifestations not only in the past, not only among ourselves. We must reject them everywhere and among all peoples. We must be the standard bearers of opposition to racism in all its forms and manifestations. Nazism was not only a German phenomenon. It is a general human phenomenon, and no people, and I stress *no people*, is immune to it.[33]

Yehoshua's emphasis on 'no people' was, of course, aimed at his fellow Jews who believe that they and their co-religionists are incapable of engaging in racism or, even more importantly, are justified in doing so. 'We must bear in mind', he continued

> that our having been victims does not accord us any special moral standing. The victim does not become virtuous for having become a victim. Although the Holocaust inflicted a horrible injustice on us, it did not grant us a certificate of everlasting righteousness. The murderers were amoral, the victims were not made moral. To be moral you must behave ethically. The test of that is daily and constant.[34]

Those on the far left of the political spectrum were convinced that the government had failed miserably. In order to drive their message home, they compared its actions and policies vis-à-vis the Palestinians to Nazi Germany's treatment of the Jews. To take the most blatant example of this kind of rhetoric: In Hanoch Levin's 'satirical cabaret', *The Patriot*, an Arab youth assumes a capitulatory pose that recalls the photograph of the terrified Jewish boy in the Warsaw Ghetto, preumably just before being shot by the Nazis. The icon remains the same but the rules have changed. Jews are no longer victims, they have become the victimizers.

Not surprisingly, those at the other end of the political spectrum, the radical right, saw the situation very differently. The Jews, they argued, were victimizing themselves. Thus, two settlers compared the Camp David Accords to the Munich agreement, and the upcoming evacuation of the Sinai Peninsula to the *Judenrein* policy of Nazi Germany. They had therefore decided to wear a yellow star. It was their way of trying to ensure 'that history would not repeat itself, and the Jewish people not have to face another terrible tragedy'.[35] Everybody, it seems, had adopted the slogan 'Never again', they just interpreted it in completely different ways.

A BLOOD LIBEL

On 16 June 1933 Dr Chaim Arlosoroff, the director of the political department of the Jewish Agency and one of the most prominent leaders of Labour Zionism was shot and killed on a Tel Aviv beach. Within a week three people, Abraham Stavsky, Zvi Rosenblatt and Aba Ahimeir were arrested. The first two were suspected of having carried out the murder, and the third one was accused of inciting them to do so. Rosenblatt and Ahimeir were released during the course of the trial, while Stavsky was found guilty and sentenced to death. However, an appeal to the Supreme Court on the grounds that his conviction had been based entirely on the testimony of Arlosoroff's wife, the only witness to the murder, was successful, and he too was released.

The case immediately became a cause célèbre because all three suspects were members of the Revisionist movement. The leaders of the Yishuv attributed the murder to a vicious incitement campaign against Labour Zionism in general and Chaim Arlosoroff in particular. The followers of Jabotinsky, in turn, accused Ben-Gurion and his colleagues of engaging in a blood libel. They contended that Labour leaders had blamed them for the murder both before the arrests were made and after all three suspects were found innocent. The accusations were a last-ditch attempt to influence the results of the upcoming elections to the Zionist Congress. The leaders of the Yishuv were prepared to do anything to hold on to the reins of power in the state in the making.

In June 1956, Menachem Begin proposed the establishment of a committee of inquiry to investigate the circumstances and accusations surrounding the murder of Chaim Arlosoroff but the motion was defeated in the Knesset. Nearly 30 years later, he made a similar proposal to the government rather than to the Israeli Parliament. The generation concerned was about to disappear and he himself would soon be retiring from public life. In addition, the publication of a book on the murder by Ben-Gurion's biographer,[36] led to a renewal of the controversy in the media. It was therefore time to set the record straight regarding the 'worst injustice ever in the history of the Jewish people besides what the gentiles did to them'.[37]

The importance that the Prime Minister attached to the establishment of the commission of inquiry was clearly apparent from the fact that it took the unprecedented step of publicizing the protocol of the cabinet meeting devoted to the issue.[38] In addition, he wrote a number of articles in the press about the extent of the blood libel against the Revisionists that took place after the murder and the renewed allegations about the incitement that allegedly caused it.[39] Menachem Begin used all his rhetorical talents to convince the government and the wider public that these matters had to be dealt with. Although the murder had occurred almost 30 years earlier it was, he insisted, still a burning issue.

The establishment of the commission of inquiry generated a great deal of criticism. Some of it was concerned with technical and legal matters. Thus Menachem Begin's opponents argued that it would be impossible to arrive at any definite conclusions after so much time had passed. The passage of time also raised the question of whether the whole issue was still of vital political importance and, therefore, a fitting subject for a commission of inquiry.[40] More frequently, however, the controversy was of a political nature. It revolved around the reasons why Menachem Begin was so intent on setting up the commission and the deleterious effects it would have on an already deeply divided society.

Critics of the government's decision argued that it would lead to a reopening of old wounds and, in turn, to a heightening of passions amongst government and opposition leaders alike. This was particularly the case because the investigation of the Arlosoroff murder was likely to be a Pandora's Box. It would give rise to demands to investigate other events that had created tensions in the pre-state Yishuv.[41] Reigniting these passions would, in turn, exacerbate current conflicts between the different camps and deepen the divisions between them – 'more poison for the cup of hatred'.

The Prime Minister, his critics insisted, was less interested in rehabilitating those accused of murder than he was in whitewashing the Revisionist movement that allegedly incited them to commit it.[42] Menachem Begin had always wanted to rewrite the history of the event by shifting the emphasis from the incitement before the murder to the blood libel that followed in its wake. Now he held the reins of power, he was able to do so.[43] Allegations of 'misuse of a legitimate state instrument for partisan purposes' and attempting to 'lay down an authoritative version of history preferred by the powers-that-be' were rejected out of hand. The government, Begin insisted, was simply fulfilling its moral duty to research the facts and tell things as they really were. In an article that appeared in Israel's two most popular newspapers he attacked those who felt that,

> it is a moral duty not to search for the truth, not to investigate whether the current allegations are right or not ... and that the members of Jabotinsky's movement have to submissively accept the accusations, see them circulate and be accepted, and do nothing ...

and went on to declare:

> Gentlemen, I do not accept this morality and will not do so until my last day on this earth. I repeat my question to all those who attacked the government's decision: Did you make false accusations and also prevent an investigation? ... With regard to the renewed allegations concerning my two comrades and the entire movement through which I have served the Jewish people for 53 years, it is necessary to set up a commission of inquiry ... It is a moral duty and we will fulfil it.[44]

Menachem Begin's opponents drew attention to another negative effect of the commission of inquiry. They contended that it would, or was even intended to, deflect attention from the 'real problems' facing Israeli society. The issues raised depended, of course, on the political stance of those concerned. For some it was the war in Lebanon,[45] for others it was the retreat from Sinai. Beyond these differences of opinion though, they were all agreed on one basic point: Menachem Begin was digging up the past instead of dealing with the present. The government was using history to avoid dealing with current problems.

THE FIGHTING FAMILY

The propaganda of Etzel and Lehi, in common with that of other terrorist movements, was replete with negative depictions of the enemy. In this case, however, attention was not only paid to the external foe. The spokesmen of both movements also attacked internal opponents. They criticized the leaders of the Yishuv for accepting the League of Nations' partition plan and for their failure to take more resolute or, to be more precise, more violent action against the mandatory authorities. Both the ends that Ben-Gurion and his colleagues set themselves and the means they used to achieve them were too limited.

Despite their prodigious propaganda efforts, Etzel and Lehi failed to achieve a great deal of support. The vast majority of the Yishuv criticized their use of violence on two grounds. They rejected it as being both immoral and inexpedient. After the establishment of independence the representatives of Revisionist Zionism continued to try and persuade their fellow-countrymen of the rightness of their actions. In numerous books and pamphlets they drew attention to the fact that their exploits had cost many lives,[46] and claimed that they were the major factor in the 'expulsion' of the British from the Holy Land. Those who survived the campaign against the mandatory authorities hailed its martyrs for their willingness to die in the struggle for independence and the contribution they made to achieve it.

After the upheaval in 1977, Likud leaders continued and even intensified the effort to legitimate the two movements associated with Revisionist Zionism. Having assumed the reins of power they had more means at their disposal to do so. Very soon after taking office, Menachem Begin suggested marking Israel's 30th anniversary with a veterans' parade that would include, *inter alia*, those who fought in the Haganah, Etzel and Lehi. The general idea was acceptable but it did not come to fruition. Begin insisted on there being parity of numbers between the different movements and that he, as Prime Minister, would lead the parade. Labour heads, however, were of the opinion that the number of participants and the order in which they marched should be in accordance with the relative size of the movements during the struggle against the British. They saw no reason why the present balance of power between the two major strands within Zionism should influence the representation of the past. Since the government and opposition could not reach an agreement on this issue the idea of the parade was dropped.[47]

Subsequent attempts to 'rectify past injustices' included the issuing of a special souvenir sheet of stamps to commemorate 'the martyrs of the struggle for Israeli independence'. Of the 20 fighters honoured, nine belonged to Etzel and three to Lehi. The much larger Haganah was clearly under-represented. In addition, members of the two movements associated with Revisionist Zionism were made eligible for, and actually received, citations as Fighters for the Establishment of the State of Israel. Henceforth, they were to be regarded as an integral part of the struggle for independence. They were no longer beyond the pale.[48]

Members of the 'fighting family' took the initiative in setting up museums to commemorate their contribution to the establishment of the state. Lehi did so in 1981 in the house of its revered leader Avraham (Yair) Stern. Etzel followed suit two years later by building one in Jaffa to honour 41 of its fighters who were killed in the capture of the city – a battle that the museum guide described as 'one of the fiercest in the War of Independence', and claimed that the Etzel had played a decisive role in it. Significantly, both exhibitions soon came under the jurisdiction of the Ministry of Defence – another sign that the two movements had lost their pariah status and achieved recognition for the role they played in the establishment of the state.

Opposition spokesmen did not accept the Likud reading of the past. Politicians and publicists alike made invidious comparisons between 'the bombastic and high fallutin words' of Revisionist leaders and the military and settlement achievements of Labour Zionism. In many instances, the critics took this line of argument a step further. They claimed that not only did Etzel and Lehi's resort to violence fail to make a significant contribution to the establishment of the state; it also had a negative impact. Many of their actions hindered rather than helped the Jewish cause.

Government critics also drew attention to the detrimental effect that Etzel and Lehi were having on current Israeli politics. Mention has already been made of the connection they drew between the two movements and contemporary street violence. Not surprisingly, however, this criticism was most frequently made with regard to the Jewish Underground. 'The arguments used by the accused and their supporters', one columnist contended,

> are strikingly similar to those employed by the Irgun Zva Leumi and Lohamei Herut Yisrael. Then it was the Jewish Agency and the Haganah, its official defence organization, that were accused of failing to hit back at Arabs; today, ironically, the same charges are made against the survivors and successors of the Etzel and Lehi ... These falsifications are of fundamental importance in creating the background for the ideology of today's terrorism. They legitimize the view that unrepresentative groups are entitled to perpetuate acts of far-reaching consequences in defiance of the properly constituted national authorities.[49]

Rewriting history, the government critics argued, was one of the reasons why it was repeating itself.

LESSONS OF THE PAST

The historical events discussed in this chapter differ with regard to both the nature of the Jewish involvement in violence and the kind of response they engendered. In some instances the Jews were the perpetrators of violence, in others they were its victims. In certain cases the debate was initiated by the government, in others the Likud simply responded or did not participate at all. However, the controversies had one thing in common – they were concerned, above all, with the present. The debates about the past provided a convenient way of trying to legitimate and/or delegitimate the current actions of the Likud government and the ideology on which they were based.

Menachem Begin and his colleagues' attempts at legitimation took one of two forms. They either appropriated national myths for party purposes or nationalized those that had hitherto been of a more partisan nature. Thus, the debates about Bar Kochba and Yosef Trumpeldor were a renewal of the long-standing struggle between the rival camps about the lessons to be learnt from those leaders. In contrast, the controversies about the murder of Chaim Arlosoroff and the contribution of Etzel and Lehi to the establishment of the state originated in the Likud's desire to turn its interpretation of events into the official one. The new government was intent on controlling the past as well as the present and the future.

The mnemonic battles both mirrored and influenced the conflicts between the rival camps. They each led to a deepening of the existing divisions within Israeli society. Paradoxically, however, the fact that history was such a contested terrain indicates the extent to which the protagonists shared the same root paradigms. Otherwise they would not be inclined, or even able, to debate the lessons of the Jewish past. Without this common background there would be no basis or reason for dialogue between the rival camps.

In each debate though, there were those who rejected the resort to history. They did not object to a particular reading of the past. Their criticism was of a more general nature. In certain instances, analogies between events that occurred in the diaspora or the Yishuv and those taking place in a sovereign Jewish state were deemed inappropriate. In other cases, those who made comparisons with the past were blamed for diverting attention, wittingly or unwittingly, from present problems. Turning to the past, it was argued, hindered, rather than helped to understand the current situation and/or to deal with it in a constructive manner.

NOTES

1. Shmuel Almog, *Zionism and History: The Rise of a New Jewish Consciousness* (Jerusalem: Magnes Press, 1987), p. 14.
2. Harkabi first addressed the issue in the weekend supplement of *Ma'ariv*. Because of the public interest it engendered, he expanded the article into a monograph and then a book on the subject. The latter was subsequently translated into English under the title *The Bar Kochba Syndrome: Risk and Realism in International Politics* (Chappaque, NY: Rossel Books, 1993).
3. This is particularly interesting in light of the fact that Menachem Begin himself referred to the revolt against the Roman Empire in support of his argument for certain kinds of restraint in the arms struggle against the British mandate. For further details see David C. Rapoport, 'Terror and the Messiah: An Ancient Experience and Some Modern Parallels', in David C. Rapoport and Yonah Alexander (eds), *The Morality of Terrorism: Religious and Secular Justifications* (New York: Pergamon Press, 1982), pp. 31–3.
4. On several occasions Harkabi added the rider 'with the exception of the Holocaust of European Jewry'.
5. Harkabi, *Bar Kochba Syndrome*, pp. 101–14.
6. Ibid., pp. xiii–xix.
7. Ibid., pp. 165–86.

8. Ironically this stance is a classic example of what Harkabi referred to earlier as the romanticization of the human factor. For further details see Yehoshafat Harkabi 'From the Guerilla Fighter to the Guerilla War', in Yehoshafat Harkabi (ed.), *On Guerilla* (Tel Aviv: Ma'arachot, 1983; in Hebrew), p. 30.
9. *Ma'ariv*, 17 October 1980.
10. Israel Eldad, *A Controversy: Our Perceptions of the Second Temple and of Bar-Kochba's Revolt* (Jerusalem: Van Leer Jerusalem Foundation, 1982; in Hebrew), pp. 16–17.
11. *Ma'ariv*, 17 October 1980.
12. Eldad, *Controversy*, p. 83.
13. For a description of the various criticisms made of the reburial ceremony see Myron J. Aronoff, 'Establishing Authority: The Memorialization of Jabotinsky and the Burial of Bar Kochba's Bones in Israel under the Likud', in Myron J. Aronoff (ed.), *The Frailty of Authority* (New Brunswick, NJ: Transaction Books, 1986), pp. 116–20. A particularly interesting one that he does not relate to was Yossi Sarid's contention that the entire operation was designed 'to deflect attention from the blood of the present to the bones of the past'.
14. Quoted in Aronoff, 'Establishing Authority', pp. 121–2.
15. One historian, however, attributed the popularity of the Tel Hai myth to the fact that it was 'the embodiment of the historical reality of a people that dwells alone'. He described Trumpeldor and his followers as 'a small group of fighters under siege, in a small island surrounded by enemies seeking to kill them'. As such they typified 'the fate that God prepared for the people of Israel throughout the generations'. For further details of this argument see Joseph Nedava, 'Jabotinsky and the Tel Hai Affair', *Hauma* 55 (September 1978), p. 371.
16. Betar was the last stronghold of Bar Kochba's revolt against the Romans. However, it is also an acronym for Brit Yosef Trumpeldor (the Yosef Trumpeldor Association). In order to achieve this double meaning the Revisionists changed the Hebrew spelling of Trumpeldor's name (from the Hebrew letter tet to tav) to fit the spelling of the ancient site.
17. Yael Zerubavel, *Recovered Roots: Collective Memory and the Making of Israeli National Tradition* (Chicago, IL: University of Chicago Press, 1985), pp. 167–77.
18. Nakdimon Rogel, *Tel Hai: A Front Without A Home Front* (Tel Aviv: Yariv/Hadar, 1979; in Hebrew).
19. Yigal Elam, 'Tel Hai and the Historian', *Nofim* 15 (Winter 1980), p. 50.
20. There were also those who warned against making this kind of historical analogy. They argued that it was impossible to compare the situation before and after the establishment of the Jewish state.
21. *Yediot Achronot*, 10 April 1979.
22. *Ha'aretz*, 6 October 1978.
23. Quoted in Robert C. Rowland, *The Rhetoric of Menachem Begin: The Myth of Redemption Through Return* (Lanham, MD: University Press of America, 1985), p. 268.
24. One observer suggested that Begin's obsession with the Holocaust was due to the fact that he suffered from the survivor syndrome, having remained alive while so many other Jews, including his close family, were killed by the Nazis and their collaborators. See Tom Segev, *The Seventh Million: The Israelis and the Holocaust* (New York: Hill & Wang, 1993), p. 396.
25. The open letter was printed in full and received extensive coverage in the Israeli press. See for instance, *Jerusalem Post*, 4 August 1982.
26. Beirut conjured up a completely different image for another survivor who staged a hunger strike outside Yad Vashem, the national Holocaust memorial in Jerusalem and issued the following statement:

> When I was a child of ten and was liberated from the concentration camp, I thought we shall never suffer again. I did not dream that we would cause suffering to others. Today we are doing just that. The Germans in Buchenwald starved us to death. Today in Jerusalem I starve myself, and this hunger of mine is no less horrific. When I hear 'filthy Arabs' I remember 'filthy Jews'. I see Beirut and I remember Warsaw.

Quoted in Amnon Rubinstein, *The Zionist Dream Revisited: From Herzl to Gush Emunim and Back* (New York: Shocken Books, 1984), p. xiii.

27. *Divrei HaKnesset* 82 (1978), p. 2014.
28. On this point see Barbie Zelizer, 'Reading the Past Against the Grain: The Shape of Memory Studies', *Critical Studies in Mass Communication* 12/2 (June 1995), pp. 222–3.
29. Menachem Begin's critics also took issue with his understanding of the Nazi period. They drew attention, for instance, to the vital role that many countries played in helping the Jews escape the horrors of the Holocaust.
30. In the Knesset debate marking the 50th anniversary of the Nazi rise to power, Yair Tzaban related to 'the completely justifiable aversion to analogies to Nazism', and suggested that they therefore be limited to 'the first stage of the journey to the abyss'. The major lesson of the Holocaust, he argued, is 'to be on constant guard against any weakening of democracy and tendency towards dictatorship'.
31. Many observers also argued that the conflict with the PLO was a political rather than a mythic one. It revolved around rival claims to the same land, and could therefore be settled by a compromise rather than having to be fought to the bitter end.
32. *Yediot Achronot*, 20 June 1980.
33. A.B. Yehoshua, *Between Right and Right. Israel: Problem or Solution?* (Garden City, NY: Doubleday, 1981), p. 11.
34. Ibid., p. 17.
35. *Yediot Achronot*, 25 March 1980.
36. Shabtai Teveth, *The Arlosoroff Murder* (Jerusalem: Schocken, 1982; in Hebrew).
37. In his concluding address at the Cabinet meeting about the commission of inquiry the Prime Minister referred to the reaction to the Arlosoroff murder as a blood libel and compared it to the controversy surrounding the Dreyfus Affair and the trial of Menachem Mendel Bailis.
38. The protocol was published in pamphlet form by the Government Information Centre under the title 'Why it is Necessary to Set up a Commission of Inquiry to Investigate the Renewed Claims and Allegations that Abraham Stavsky and Zvi Rosenblatt or One of Them took Part in the Murder of Chaim Arlosoroff'.
39. See, for instance, *Yediot Achronot*, 19 February 1982, 26 February 1982 and 19 March 1982.
40. One critic of the commission sarcastically suggested that the government should set up a similar one to investigate the circumstances surrounding the murder of Jesus, why he disappeared and where to, in order to finally dispel the suspicions that had brought so much suffering to the Jewish people over the last 2,000 years.
41. The sinking of the Irgun arms ship, the *Altalena*, was the most frequently mentioned incident in this regard. For further details of the event itself and of the response it engendered see Ehud Sprinzak, *Brother Against Brother: Violence and Extremism in Israeli Politics from Altalena to the Rabin Assassination* (New York: Free Press, 1999), pp. 17–32.
42. According to a number of observers, Menachem Begin's decision to set up the commission of inquiry was also motivated by the fact that the incitement to the murder of Chaim Arlosoroff was repeatedly mentioned in the stigma contests about verbal violence described in Chapter 4.
43. Menachem Begin was criticized for pre-empting the commission's investigation by repeatedly using the term blood libel and declaring that it was necessary to revise the existing history textbooks. In the end, the commission concluded that neither Stavsky nor Rosenblatt were guilty, but that it was impossible to say who had, in fact, committed the murder and whether it was politically motivated. See *Commission of Inquiry into the Murder of Dr. Chaim Arlosoroff, Final Report* (State of Israel: Jerusalem 1985; in Hebrew), p. 200.
44. *Ma'ariv* and *Yediot Achronot*, 19 March 1982.
45. One member of the Commission resigned in protest against the government's procrastination in setting up a similar one to investigate the Sabra and Shatilla massacre.
46. This argument provides a classic example of the assertion that 'it is the ownership of military casualties that provides a group's most dramatic claim of centrality in Israel's society'. On this point see Myron J. Aronoff, 'Myths, Symbols and Rituals of the Emerging State', in Lawrence J. Silbestein (ed.), *New Perspectives in Israeli History: The Early Years of the State* (New York: New York University Press, 1991), p. 181.
47. The veterans' march was a compromise idea that Menachem Begin suggested after his initial plan for a full-scale military parade was dropped because of widespread public criticism.
48. Likud leaders tried to make a clear distinction between the actions of Etzel and Lehi and

those of the PLO. Thus, Dr Eli Tavin, an Etzel veteran and the head of the World Zionist Organization Department of Education and Culture in the Diaspora, organized an interuniversity conference on underground movements that was designed to find a scientific basis for the dichotomy between freedom fighters and terrorists. The proceedings of the meeting were subsequently published and used in Israeli propaganda campaigns abroad.

49. *Jerusalem Post*, 29 May 1984.

Conclusions

CENTRE AND PERIPHERY

The upheaval of 1977 was much more than a change of government; it signified the end of 30 years of Labour dominance. Menachem Begin and his colleagues were no longer pariahs. They had moved from the periphery to the very centre of the Israeli body politic. However, the struggle for political legitimacy continued unabated. In fact, the first period of Likud rule was characterized by a particularly fierce rivalry between the two major political blocs. Government and opposition leaders alike stepped up their efforts to legitimate their own policies and ideologies, and to delegitimate those of their most long-standing and fervent rivals.

The allegations against the government bore a striking resemblance to those directed against the leaders of Revisionist Zionism during the period of the Yishuv. Thus, the criticism of the War in Lebanon was very similar to the attack on Etzel and Lehi for not upholding the official policy of restraint vis-à-vis the British mandatory authorities. The charges concerning verbal violence resembled the accusations of incitement made after the murder of Chaim Arlosoroff. Clearly the re-ideologization of Israeli society led to a repetition of earlier controversies. Protagonists of all persuasions revived the arguments of yesteryear.

The stigma contests during the period of Likud rule not only resembled previous struggles between Labour and Revisionist Zionism. The earlier disputes were often referred to in the contemporary ones. Opposition leaders recalled past incidents of violence in order to show that the current actions and inaction of the Likud were part of a long-standing pattern. Menachem Begin and his colleagues responded in kind. They portrayed Labour attitudes as a repeat of past patterns. Both sides tried to make the same point: that nothing at all had changed.[1]

This attempt to create a feeling of déjà vu must not be allowed to hide the important changes that occurred between the two sets of stigma contests. The pre-state Yishuv developed into the State of Israel and the reins of power moved from the heirs of Ben-Gurion to his most vehement opponents. Consequently, the latest round of Labour allegations were directed against the leaders of a sovereign state. The Likud government was condemned for its use of force, and for failing to prevent others from resorting to violence or even encouraging them to do so. Menachem Begin and his colleagues had to defend themselves against accusations of being both the perpetrators of, and auxiliaries to violence.[2]

Although these two kinds of controversies have been analyzed as separate entities there was, in fact, a great deal of interaction between them. Government critics, for instance, claimed that the state use of force in the territories or in Lebanon led to the violence of non-state actions against Jews and Arabs alike.[3] They also argued that the glorification of dissident violence against the Roman and/or British Empires helped pave the way for the use of force by the Likud administration. One kind of violence allegedly led to another. They were inextricably intertwined.

This argument was often taken a step further. Government critics not only claimed that state and non-state violence amplified each other; they also attributed both to the same causes. Thus, the use of both kinds of force was imputed to Menachem Begin and Ariel Sharon, and/or the ideology they represented. It was their personalities and policies that were ultimately to blame.

The tendency to attribute diverse kinds of violence to the same causes, and the interaction between the various disputes, led to a convergence between them. The different controversies between the two major political blocs coalesced into a more general concern about the increase in violence in Israeli society. As in the United States, the United Kingdom and elsewhere, it gave rise to a widespread moral panic.[4] However, the response also differed from that in other countries in one important respect. It concentrated on the centre rather than on the periphery of the body politic. Those at the helm of the state were the focus of attention.

The disputes between the two major Zionist camps were paralleled by a series of controversies between ultra-orthodox Judaism and

Zionism as a whole. The Haredi critique of the violence on the streets, for instance, was by no means a new phenomenon. It was essentially similar to the earlier attack on the assassination of the noted ultra-orthodox leader, Dr Isaac De-Hahn, by the Haganah in 1929.[5] Once again, therefore, prior examples of violence were cited in support of the assertion that contemporary incidents were just the most recent manifestation of a more basic problem. Secular Zionism was, and always has been, responsible for the violence in Israeli society.

Both the content and the target of the Haredi attack were much broader than that of the secular government critics. Ultra-orthodox leaders related to a wider variety of social problems rather than just to the different kinds of violence,[6] and they lambasted Zionism as a whole instead of one particular version of it. However, the Haredi allegations were exactly the same as those of the Labour Party in one important respect. They were also directed against those at the centre rather than the periphery of the body politic.

It is to the reasons for this pattern that we must now turn our attention. Before doing so, however, it is necessary to place the Israeli experience in a broader context. This will help us understand the lines of cleavage and bones of contention in the Israeli stigma contests, and to make a number of conjectures about the situation beyond the confines of the Jewish state.

DAY AND NIGHT

Faced with an inherently chaotic world, human beings experience an acute need to make everything appear orderly and meaningful. They do so by creating a symbolic universe that 'integrates different provinces of meaning and encompasses the institutional order in a symbolic totality'.[7] Because it is self-confirming, the fact that this canopy of meaning is humanly constructed tends to be forgotten. After all, the validity of any symbolic universe is 'proven' each time the categories embedded in it are used to view reality. It hardens and thickens, and gradually assumes the appearance of objective reality – it becomes a world-taken-for-granted.

Paradoxically, however, any symbolic universe is always highly precarious. The mere appearance of an alternative one demonstrates that it is less than inevitable; that there is another way of making order out of chaos. Berger and Luckman captured the menacing nature of this threat in a powerful analogy. Alternative constructions of reality, they insist:

> constitute the most acute threat to taken-for-granted routinized existence in society. If one conceives of the latter as the 'daylight side' of human life, then they constitute a 'night side' that keeps lurking ominously on the periphery of everyday consciousness. Just because the 'night side' has its own reality, often enough of a sinister kind, it is a constant threat to the taken-for-granted, matter-of-fact, 'sane' reality of life in society. The thought keeps suggesting itself that perhaps the bright reality of everyday life is but an illusion, to be swallowed up at any moment by the howling nightmare of the other 'night-side' reality.[8]

Human beings employ a wide variety of universe-maintenance mechanisms to ward off this anomic terror and retain a feeling that 'everything makes sense'.[9] One way of doing so – therapy – concentrates on keeping actual and potential deviants within the accepted definition of reality.[10] Of particular interest to this study, though, is the alternative method of nihilation.[11] Rather than trying to keep everyone within the universe in question, this mechanism attempts to conceptually liquidate everything beyond its boundaries. While the universe maintenance may take many forms the aim is always the same – the delegitimation of rivals and the legitimation of self.

Universe maintenance is, of course, a universal phenomenon. It occurred even in pre-modern societies that were characterized by a monopolistic tradition, usually of a religious nature – by what Berger aptly called a sacred canopy.[12] It has become much more widespread, however, since this hegemony came to an end. As a result of the secularization of consciousness, most individuals look at the world without the benefit of traditional, or any other religious interpretations. Even those who retain the old beliefs and practices do so in a very different way from their pre-modern counterparts. Their religious allegiance is voluntary, a matter of choice rather than destiny.[13]

The predicament of *homo religioso* may be particularly acute in this respect. However, he is by no means *sui generis*; he differs in degree rather than in kind from his secular counterparts. One of the major characteristics of modernity is the plurality of life-worlds, so that contemporary man is forced to choose between a bewildering array of alternatives. The threat of chaos is more pervasive than ever. Modern man is engaged in a constant attempt to defend his worldview by liquidating competing views of reality. In order to retain his sanity he tries to place all alternative symbolic universes beyond the pale.[14] Israel is no exception to this situation. In fact, it provides classic examples of both secularization in particular and the plurality of life worlds in general. In this respect, at least, the Jewish state is a modern society par excellence.

With the advent of Jewish nationality, traditional Jews were confronted with an avowedly secular and dogmatically anti-religious alternative. Although Zionism has become less strident with the passage of time, the leaders of the ultra-orthodox community still feel that their secular counterparts are actively engaged in a 'holy war' against God and His commandments. They employ the twin strategies of withdrawal from and conquest of the surrounding society in order to avoid and counter the deleterious effects of this anti-religious crusade respectively. These policies are backed up by a spirited critique of both the ideological tenets of secular Zionism and its deleterious consequences.

Contrary to the ultra-orthodox view of things, however, secular Zionism is not a homogeneous entity. The brief analysis of the Israeli body politic in Chapter 1 provides clear indication of the fact that the Zionist movement has always been 'a family of visions and a federation of dreams'.[15]

> Whereas all Zionist parties shared common assumptions, each interpreted the various Zionist myths through its ideological perspective ... The ideological interpretations by the various political movements constitute competing visions of a shared overall symbolic universe ... Within the general Zionist framework, socialist, revisionist and religious Zionism have competed with one another for power and the right to claim their vision to be the *true* interpretation of *the* Zionist vision.[16]

The competition can, and does in fact, assume a wide variety of forms. Clearly, however, engaging in the kinds of controversies described in this book plays a vital role in the struggle for legitimacy. Protagonists of all persuasions join the issue over the state and/or non-state use of force as part of their attempt to show that they are 'the real thing'.

LINES OF CLEAVAGE

People use universe-maintenance mechanisms if and when they feel that their life-world is jeopardized and can no longer be taken for granted. As Edwin Schur has pointed out, 'the concept of perceived threat provides a key link between the overall or basic boundary-maintaining function of deviance-defining and the emergence of particular collective definitions of deviance within specific social contexts'.[17] Sociologists have therefore singled out the volume of deviance,[18] the offenders' motives,[19] and other variables that in their opinion heighten the threat potential of deviance and thereby increase the need to change or nihilate those engaged in it.

Berger and Luckmann themselves argued that intersocietal challenges are more threatening than intrasocietal ones, because they originate in an alternative symbolic universe with an 'official' tradition whose taken-for-granted objectivity is equal to one's own.[20] According to Ben-Yehuda, however, exactly the opposite is the case. He contends that a challenge coming from outside a particular symbolic universe is easier to cope with since it can be interpreted as representing a different and alien world. In contrast, an internal challenge is considered more threatening. In such cases 'it is the center's moral right to rule and its moral hierarchy and legitimacy that are being challenged'.[21]

The present research is also concerned with the question of how the place of origin of alternative versions of reality influence their perceived threat to one's own life-world. It suggests, however, that it is not possible to make broad generalizations in this regard. The site of the most serious threat varies from one society to another and, within each one, from one period to another. It depends on the nature of the body politic at a particular point in time.

The centrality of controversies between the different camps in Israel is due to its highly fragmented political culture.[22] The Jewish state is characterized by deep ideological divisions between Zionists and non-Zionists and, even more importantly, between different visions of the Zionist dream. Protagonists of all persuasions feel that their life-world is endangered by those of the rival camps and they therefore try their utmost to nihilate them. This is particularly the case during periods of ideological polarization. At such times the threat posed by political opponents is perceived as even more severe than usual, and the need to delegitimate them increases accordingly.

Of course, Israel is by no means unique in this regard. Other consociational democracies[23] are characterized by a high degree of political fragmentation, and political divisions exist in all democratic societies. They differ in degree rather than in kind. Consequently, the sort of controversies described in this book also occur elsewhere. They have not been studied, though, because of a widely held misperception regarding the contours of modern societies.

Conceiving of society in terms of a centre and periphery has led to an almost total preoccupation with the disputes between them. Clearly, however, this is a rather simplistic image of reality. Modern societies are best understood as a number of competing symbolic universes within a shared overall one. Whether the latter is envisaged as the overlapping part of the different life-worlds or as a completely separate one the end result is the same. There are always two kinds of controversies. Adherents of the rival symbolic universes simultaneously engage in battles against each other, and in a joint struggle against a common foe. They are enemies and allies at one and the same time.

The balance between the two kinds of disputes depends on which part of the protagonists' life-world is felt to be the most severely threatened by alternative views of reality. Extrapolating from the Israeli experience, it is hypothesized that the greater the degree of ideological polarization in a particular society, the more central the role played by the different kinds of polemic between the rival camps. The greater the degree of consensus, the more the protagonists can, and will turn their attention, to those who constitute a threat to the shared worldview of the society in question.

This hypothesis does not only relate to the overall balance between controversies in a society at a particular point in time. It can also be applied to single cases of deviance by non-state actors. Thus, the balance between the two kinds of nihilation – of the perpetrators themselves and their alleged auxiliaries – reflects the relative danger that they constitute to those concerned. Once again, the perceived threat is the major factor in determining the response.

BONES OF CONTENTION

Heavily influenced by the state-centred paradigm concerning the legitimate use of force, most scholars have concentrated their attention on the controversies surrounding non-state actors. Paradoxically, however, these studies indicate that those concerned invariably portray their resort to violence as a response to the prior actions or inaction of the state. Their self-legitimation is based, to a large extent at least, on the delegitimation of those holding the reins of power. The disputes about non-state actors and the state are inextricably intertwined.

Israel is no exception to this rule. Those non-state actors, both Israeli and Palestinian, who resorted to violence accepted responsibility for their behaviour but placed the blame on the government. Their actions, they insisted, were a legitimate response to the failings or inequities of the powers-that-be. However, the criticism of the state was by no means limited to those who actually resorted to violence against it. Both the parliamentary and extra-parliamentary opponents of the government attacked Menachem Begin and his colleagues for their own actions and for their failure to prevent those of their more rabid followers. They also focused on the sins of commission and omission of the powers-that-be.

As has already been pointed out, disputes about violence were by no means a new phenomenon in Israel. The state and non-state use of force are a long-standing bone of contention, between Zionists and non-Zionists and, even more importantly, between the different Zionist camps. This can be explained, in part at least, in terms of the ideological foundations of the Jewish state.[24] However, the fact that violence is a major issue in many other countries suggests the need to find an explanation of a more general nature.

On the basis of his study of wayward puritans in the Massachusetts Bay Colony, Kai Erikson contended that every society has its own special set of boundaries and, therefore, its own characteristic style of deviance. 'Deviant behavior', he argued, 'appears in a community at exactly the points where it is most feared'.[25] Continuing this line of thought, the present study suggests that the disquiet may be generated by a particular mode of operation rather than a certain kind of behaviour. Violence of any form, and not the infraction of a specific law, is the major cause of concern.[26]

This focus on the use of physical force is due to the fact that it constitutes the major distinguishing feature of the state. Because it cannot be differentiated from other associations in terms of its ends, but only on the basis of the unique means that the government has at its disposal to achieve them, the issue of violence provides the perfect grounds for delegitimating those who hold the reins of power. Their resort to force and/or their failure to prevent others from doing so furnish the ideal basis for nihilating the powers-that-be. They are the ultimate *causus belli*, the bone of contention par excellence.

NOTES

1. Both sides referred to the violent incidents that occurred during the period of Likud rule in subsequent stigma contests between them. This was particularly the case in the debate before and after the assassination of Yitzhak Rabin in November 1995.
2. Some of the accounts may have been generated by a process of internal questioning rather than in response to external criticism. However, to the extent that the self-reflection was

engaged in openly, the end result was the same – a public debate about the government's role as perpetrators of, or auxiliaries to, violence.
3. On several occasions they claimed that the state use of force led to ordinary as well as political violence. However, this argument has not been dealt with in the present book.
4. For an explanation of this concept and a review of the relevant literature see Erich Goode and Nachman Ben-Yehuda, 'Moral Panics: Culture, Politics and Social Construction', *Annual Review of Sociology* 20 (1994), pp. 149–71.
5. For further details of the Haredi response to the assassination see Menachem Friedman, *Society and Religion: The Non-Zionist Orthodox in Eretz-Israel 1918–1936* (Jerusalem: Yad Itzhak Ben-Zvi Publications, 1977; in Hebrew), pp. 230–52.
6. This is due to the fact that they resorted to a vacuum rather than a consistency image when dealing with the issue of causal responsibility. These concepts are developed in Gerald Cromer, *The Writing was On The Wall: Constructing Political Deviance in Israel* (Ramat Gan: Bar Ilan University Press, 1998), pp. 136–9.
7. Peter Berger and Thomas Luckmann, *The Social Construction of Reality: A Treatise in the Sociology of Knowledge* (Garden City, NY: Doubleday, 1966), p. 88.
8. Ibid., p. 91.
9. Ibid., pp. 96–107.
10. This particular universe-maintenance mechanism is also referred to as normalization because it includes attempts to eradicate deviant behaviour by coercion as well as rehabilitative means. See Robert A. Scott, 'A Proposed Framework for Analyzing Deviance as a Property of Social Order', in Robert A. Scott and Jack Douglas (eds), *Theoretical Perspectives on Deviance* (New York: Basic Books, 1972), pp. 25–6.
11. Berger and Luckmann, *Social Construction of Reality*, pp. 114–16.
12. Peter L. Berger, *The Sacred Canopy: Elements of a Sociological Theory of Religion* (Garden City, NY: Anchor Books, 1969).
13. Ibid., pp. 108–9.
14. Peter L. Berger, Brigitte Berger and Hansfried Keller, *The Homeless Mind: Modernization and Consciousness* (Harmondsworth: Penguin Books, 1974), pp. 62–77.
15. Amos Oz, *Under This Blazing Light* (Tel Aviv: Sifriat Hapoalim, 1979; in Hebrew), p. 92.
16. Myron J. Aronoff, 'The Origins of Israeli Political Culture', in Ehud Sprinzak and Larry Diamond (eds), *Israeli Democracy Under Stress* (Boulder, CO: Lynne Rienner, 1993), pp. 49–51. Italics in original.
17. Edwin M. Schur, *The Politics of Deviance: Stigma Contests and the Uses of Power* (Englewood Cliffs, NJ: Prentice Hall, 1980), pp. 24–5.
18. Kai T. Erikson, *Wayward Puritans: A Study in the Sociology of Deviance* (New York: John Wiley & Sons, 1966), pp. 23–7.
19. Joseph R. Gusfield, 'Moral Passage: The Symbolic Process in Public Designations of Deviance', *Social Problems* 15/2 (Fall 1967), pp. 178–82.
20. Berger and Luckmann, *Social Construction of Reality*, p. 107.
21. Nachman Ben-Yehuda, *The Politics and Morality of Deviance: Moral Panics, Drug Abuse, Deviant Sciences and Reversed Stigmatization* (Albany, NY: State University of New York Press, 1990), p. 72.
22. Gabriel Almond, 'Comparative Political Systems', *Journal of Politics* 18/3 (August 1956), pp. 403–8.
23. Arend Lijphart, 'Consocientional Democracy', *World Politics* 21/2 (January 1969).
24. On this point see Anita Shapira, *Land and Power: The Zionist Resort to Force 1881–1948* (New York: Oxford University Press, 1992).
25. Erikson, *Wayward Puritans*, pp. 19–23.
26. The actual form of violence, however, is influenced by the context in which it occurs. Different kinds of sacred terror, for instance, reflected the distinguishing characteristics of the religions in which they originated. See David C. Rapoport, 'Fear and Trembling: Terrorism in the Religious Traditions', *American Political Science Review* 78/3 (September 1984), pp. 658–77.

Bibliography

NEWSPAPERS AND PERIODICALS

Al Hamishmar
Davar
Ha'aretz
Ha'ir
Hadashot
Hamodia
IDF Journal
Jerusalem Post
Ma'ariv
Nekuda
Palestine
Palestine Altara
Palestine Perspectives
Palestine Sheun
Yediot Achronot

BOOKS AND ARTICLES

Abramov, Zalman S., *Perpetual Dilemma: Jewish Religion in the Jewish State* (Rutherford, NJ: Fairleigh Dickenson University Press, 1976).

Almog, Shmuel, *Zionism and History: The Rise of a New Jewish Consciousness* (Jerusalem: Magnes Press, 1987).

Almond, Gabriel, 'Comparative Political Systems', *Journal of Politics*, 18/3 (August 1956), pp. 391–409.

Apter, David E., 'Democracy and Emancipatory Movements: Notes for a Theory of Inversionary Discourse', *Development and Change* 23/3

(July 1992), pp. 139–73.

Aretxaga, Begona, 'Striking With Hunger: Cultural Meanings of Political Violence in Northern Ireland', in Kay Warren (ed.), *The Violence Within: Cultural and Political Opposition in Divided Nations* (Boulder, CO: Westview Press, 1993), pp. 219–53.

Arian, Alan and Barnes, Samuel H., 'The Dominant Party System: A Neglected Model of Democratic Stability', *Journal of Politics* 36/3 (August 1974), pp. 592–614.

Arieli, Yehoshua, 'Israeli Democracy Facing the Test of the War in Lebanon', in Rubik Rosenthal (ed.), *Lebanon: The Other War* (Tel Aviv: Sifriat Hapoalim, 1983; in Hebrew), pp. 155–79.

Aronoff, Myron J., 'Establishing Authority: The Memorialization of Jabotinsky and the Burial of Bar Kochba's Bones in Israel under the Likud', in Myron J. Aronoff (ed.), *The Frailty of Authority* (New Brunswick, NJ: Transaction Books, 1986), pp. 105–30.

Aronoff, Myron J. 'Myths, Symbols and Rituals of the Emerging State', in Laurence J. Silberstein (ed.), *New Perspectives in Israeli History: The Early Years of the State* (New York: New York University Press, 1991), pp. 175–92.

Aronoff, Myron J., 'The Origins of Israeli Political Culture', in Ehud Sprinzak and Larry Diamond (eds), *Israeli Democracy Under Stress* (Boulder, CO: Lynne Rienner, 1993), pp. 47–63.

Bar-Tal, Daniel, 'The Monopoly of Patriotism', in Daniel Bar-Tal and Ervin Staub (eds), *Patriotism in the Lives of Individuals and Nations* (Chicago, IL: Nelson Hall, 1977), pp. 246–70.

Barnur, Coresh, 'Rhetoric in the Cycle of Terror: The Coverage of the Coastal Road Incident and the Litani Operation in the Israeli and Palestinian Press' (unpublished MA thesis, Bar Ilan University, Ramat Gan, 1998; in Hebrew).

Barzilai, Gad, *Wars, Internal Conflicts and Political Order: A Jewish Democracy in the Middle East* (Albany, NY: State University of New York Press, 1996).

Ben-Yehuda, Nachman, *The Politics and Morality of Deviance: Moral Panics, Drug Abuse, Deviant Sciences and Reversed Stigmatization* (Albany, NY: State University of New York Press, 1990).

Berger, Peter L., *The Sacred Canopy: Elements of a Sociological Theory of Religion* (Garden City, NY: Anchor Books, 1969).

Berger, Peter L. and Luckmann, Thomas, *The Social Construction of Reality: A Treatise in the Sociology of Knowledge* (Garden City, NY: Doubleday, 1966).

Berger, Peter L., Berger, Brigitte and Keller, Hansfried, *The Homeless Mind: Modernization and Consciousness* (Harmondsworth: Penguin Books, 1974).
Best, Joel, 'Rhetoric in Claims Making: Constructing the Missing Children Problem', *Social Problems* 24/2 (April 1987), pp. 101–21.
Bruner, Edward M. and Gorfain, Phyllis, 'Dialogic Narration and the Paradoxes of Massada', in Edward M. Bruner (ed.), *Text, Play and Story: The Construction and Reconstruction of Self and Society* (Washington, DC: American Ethnological Society, 1984), pp. 56–79.
Cohen, Stanley, *States of Denial: Knowing About Atrocities and Suffering* (Cambridge: Polity, 2001).
Commission of Inquiry into the Murder of Dr Chaim Arlosoroff, Final Report (State of Israel: Jerusalem, 1985; in Hebrew).
Cromer, Gerald, 'The Creation of Others: A Case Study of Meir Kahane and His Opponents', in Silberstein, Laurence J. and Cohn, Robert L. (eds), *The Other in Jewish Thought and History: Constructions of Jewish Culture and Identity* (New York: New York University Press, 1994), pp. 281–304.
Cromer, Gerald, 'Secularism is the Root of All Evil: The Haredi Response to Crime and Delinquency', *International Journal of Group Tensions* 26/2 (Summer 1996), pp. 104–21.
Cromer, Gerald, *The Writing was on the Wall: Constructing Political Deviance in Israel* (Ramat Gan: Bar Ilan University Press, 1998).
Cromer, Gerald, *Narratives of Violence* (Aldershot: Ashgate, 2001).
Deshen, Shlomo, 'Doves, Hawks and Anthropology: The Israeli Debate on Middle Eastern Settlement Proposals', in Gisli Pallson (ed.), *Beyond Boundaries: Understanding Translation and Anthropological Discourse* (Oxford: Berg, 1993), pp. 58–74.
Duverger, Maurice, *Political Parties: Their Organization and Activity in the Modern State* (London: Methuen, 1964).
Eban, Abba, 'The Duty to Oppose', in Hillel Schenker (ed.), *After Lebanon: The Israeli–Palestinian Connection* (New York: Pilgrim Press, 1983), pp. 365–9.
Eitan, Rafael, *The Story of a Soldier* (Tel Aviv: Ma'ariv, 1985; in Hebrew).
Elam, Yigal, 'Tel Hai and the Historian', *Nofim* 15 (Winter 1980), pp. 9–19.
Elazar, Daniel, J., 'Israel's Compound Polity', in Ernest Krausz (ed.), *Politics and Society in Israel* (New Brunswick, NJ: Transaction Books, 1985), pp. 43–80.

Elazar, Daniel J. and Sandler, Shmuel, 'The Two-Bloc System: A New Development in Israeli Politics', in Daniel J. Elazar and Shmuel Sandler (eds), *Israel's Odd Couple: The 1984 Elections and the National Unity Government* (Detroit, MI: Wayne University Press, 1990), pp. 11–24.

Eldad, Israel, *A Controversy: Our Perceptions of the Second Temple and of Bar-Kochba's Revolt* (Jerusalem: Van Leer Jerusalem Foundation, 1982; in Hebrew).

Erikson, Kai T., *Wayward Puritans: A Study in the Sociology of Deviance* (New York: John Wiley & Sons, 1966).

Etzion, Yehuda, 'From the Laws of Existence to the Laws of Destiny', *Nekuda* 75 (6 July 1984), pp. 22–7.

Etzion, Yehuda, *The Temple Mount* (Jerusalem: Caspi, 1985; in Hebrew).

Feagin, Joe R. and Hohn, Harlan, *Ghetto Revolts: The Politics of Violence in American Cities* (New York: Macmillan, 1973).

Fein, Leonard J., *Politics in Israel* (Boston, MA: Little Brown & Co., 1967).

Feldman, Shai and Rechnitz-Kejner, Heda, *Deception, Concensus and War: Israel in Lebanon* (Boulder, CO: Westview Press, 1984).

Friedman, Menachem, *Society and Religion: The Non-Zionist Orthodox in Eretz-Israel 1918–1936* (Jerusalem: Yad Itzhak Ben-Zvi Publications, 1977; in Hebrew).

Galnoor, Itzhak, 'Transformations in the Israeli Political System since the Yom Kippur War', in Asher Arian (ed.), *The Elections in Israel 1977* (Jerusalem: Jerusalem Academic Press, 1980), pp. 119–48.

Gerth, H.H. and Mills, C. Wright, *From Max Weber: Essays in Sociology* (New York: Oxford University Press, 1969).

Gertz, Nurith, *Capture of a Dream: National Myths in Israeli Culture* (Tel Aviv: Am Oved, 1995; in Hebrew).

Goode, Erich and Ben-Yehuda, Nachman, 'Moral Panics: Culture, Politics and Social Construction', *Annual Review of Sociology* 20 (1994), pp. 149–71.

Gusfield, Joseph R., 'Moral Passage: the Symbolic Process in Public Designations of Deviance', *Social Problems* 15/2 (Fall 1967), pp. 175–88.

Hall, Stuart, Critcher, Chas, Tony Jefferson, Clark, John and Roberts, Brian, *Policing the Crisis: Mugging, the State, and Law and Order* (London: Macmillan, 1978).

Harkabi, Yehoshafat, *The Bar Kochba Syndrome: Risk and Realism in*

International Politics (Chappaque, NY: Rossel Books, 1983).
Harkabi, Yehoshafat, 'From the Guerilla Fighter to the Guerilla War', in Yehoshafat Harkabi (ed.), *On Guerilla* (Tel Aviv: Ma'arachot, 1983; in Hebrew), pp. 11–107.
Harkabi, Yehoshafat, *Fateful Decisions* (Tel Aviv: Am Oved, 1986; in Hebrew).
Hever, Hanan and Ron, Moshe, *Fighting and Killing Without End: Political Poetry in the Lebanon War* (Tel Aviv: Kibbutz Hameuchad, 1983; in Hebrew).
Hirschman, Albert O., *The Rhetoric of Reaction: Perversity, Futility and Jeopardy* (Cambridge, MA: Harvard University Press, 1991).
Holstein, James A. and Miller, Gale,'Rethinking Victimization: An Interactional Approach to Victimology', *Symbolic Interaction* 13/1 (Spring 1990), pp. 103–22.
Horowitz, Dan and Lissak, Moshe, *Trouble in Utopia: The Overburdened Polity of Israel* (Albany, NY: State University of New York Press, 1989).
Inbar, Efraim, 'The No-Choice War Debate in Israel', *Journal of Strategic Studies* 12/1 (March 1989), pp. 22–37.
Isaac, Real Jean, *Party and Politics in Israel: Three Visions of a Jewish State* (Baltimore, MD: John Hopkins University Press, 1981).
Kahane, Meir, *They Must Go* (New York: Grosset & Dunlop, 1981).
Kahane, Meir, *Forty Years* (Miami Beach, FL: Institute of the Jewish Idea, 1983).
Koren, Alina, 'The Coverage of Land Day in the Israeli Press', *Patuach* 2 (Summer 1994), pp. 3–16.
Kotler, Yair, *Heil Kahane!* (New York: Adama Books, 1986).
Le Bon, Gustave, *The Crowd: A Study of the Popular Mind* (London: T. Fisher Unwin, 1960).
Lederman, Eliezer and Tabory, Mala, 'Criminalization of Racial Incitement in Israel', *Stanford Journal of International Law* 24/1 (Winter 1988), pp. 55–84.
Leeman, Richard W., *The Rhetoric of Terrorism and Counterterrorism* (New York: Greenwood Press, 1991).
Lehman-Wilzig, Sam N., *Stiff-Necked People, Bottle-Necked System: The Evolution and Roots of Israeli Public Protest 1949–1986* (Bloomington, IN: Indiana University Press, 1990).
Levitan, Uri, 'Four Psychological Phenomena and the War in Lebanon', in Rubik Rosenthal (ed.), *Lebanon: The Other War* (Tel Aviv: Sifriat Hapoalim, 1983; in Hebrew), pp. 145–54.

Levitte, Ariel and Tarrow, Sydney, 'The Legitimation of Excluded Parties in Dominant Party Systems', *Comparative Politics* 15/3 (April 1983), pp. 295–327.

Liebman, Charles S. and Don-Yehiya, Eliezer, *Civil Religion in Israel: Traditional Judaism and Political Culture in the Jewish State* (Berkeley, CA: University of California Press, 1983).

Lijphart, Arend, 'Consocientional Democracy', *World Politics* 21/2 (January 1969), pp. 207–25.

Linn, Ruth, *Not Shooting and Not Crying: Psychological Inquiry into Moral Disobedience* (Westport, CT: Greenwood Press, 1989).

Ne'eman, Yuval, *A Sober Policy?* (Ramat Gan: Revivim, 1984; in Hebrew).

Nedava, Joseph, 'Jabotinsky and the Tel Hai Affair', *Hauma* 55 (September 1978), pp. 366–73.

Nossek, Hillel, 'The Narrative Role of the Holocaust and the State of Israel in the Coverage of Salient Terrorist Events in the Israeli Press', *Journal of Narrative and Life History* 4/1 and 2 (1994), pp. 119–34.

O'Brien, William V., *Law and Morality in Israel's War with the PLO* (New York: Routledge, 1991).

Oz, Amos, *Under This Blazing Light* (Tel Aviv: Sifriat Hapoalim, 1979; in Hebrew).

Pfuhl, Edwin, *The Deviance Process* (New York: D. Van Nostrand, 1980).

Rabin, Yitzhak, 'The Price of Political Delusions', in *The Lebanon War: Between Protest and Compliance* (Tel Aviv: Hakibbutz Hameuchad, 1983; in Hebrew), pp. 13–22.

Rabin, Yitzhak, *The Lebanon War* (Tel Aviv: Am Oved, 1983; in Hebrew).

Rapaport, Era, *Letters from Tel Mond Prison: An Israeli Settler Defends the Act of Terror* (New York: Free Press, 1996).

Rapoport, David C. 'Terror and the Messiah: An Ancient Experience and Some Modern Parallels', in David C. Rapoport and Yonah Alexander (eds), *The Morality of Terrorism: Religious and Secular Justifications* (New York: Pergamon Press, 1982), pp. 13–42.

Rapoport, David C., 'Fear and Trembling: Terrorism in the Religious Traditions, *American Political Science Review* 78/3 (September 1984), pp. 658–77.

Rapoport, David C. and Weinberg, Leonard, 'Elections and Violence', *Terrorism and Political Violence* 12/3 and 4 (Autumn/Winter 2000), pp. 15–50.

Ravitsky, Aviezer, 'Roots of Kahanism: Consciousness and Political Reality', *Jerusalem Quarterly* 39 (1986), pp. 91–100.

Raz, Nachman, 'An Examination of Basics in the Light of War', in *The Political–Military Arena: An Examination and Critique of the War in Lebanon* (Ramat Efal: Yad Tabenkin, 1982; in Hebrew), pp. 17–22.

Riches, David,'The Phenomenon of Violence', in David Riches (ed.), *The Anthropology of Violence* (Oxford: Basil Blackwell, 1986), pp. 1–27.

Rogel, Nakdimon, *Tel Hai: A Front Without A Home Front* (Tel Aviv: Yariv/Hadar, 1979; in Hebrew).

Rosenbaum, H. Jon and Sederberg, Peter C., 'Vigilantism: An Analysis of Establishment Violence', *Comparative Politics* 6/4 (July 1974), pp. 541–70.

Rowland, Robert C. *The Rhetoric of Menachem Begin: The Myth of Redemption Through Return* (Lanham, MD: University Press of America, 1985).

Rubinstein, Amnon, *The Zionist Dream Revisited: From Herzl to Gush Emunim and Back* (New York: Shocken Books, 1984).

Schafer, Stephen, *The Political Criminal: The Problem of Morality and Crime* (New York: Free Press, 1974).

Schatzberger,Hilda, *Resistance and Tradition in Mandatory Palestine* (Ramat Gan: Bar Ilan University Press, 1985; in Hebrew).

Schiff, Ze'ev and Ya'ari, Ehud, *Israel's Lebanon War* (New York: Simon & Schuster, 1984).

Schlenker, Barry R., *Impression Management: The Self-Concept, Social Identity and Interpersonal Relations* (Monterey, CA: Brooks/Cole, 1980).

Schmid, Alex P. and de Graaf, Jenny, *Violence as Communication: Insurgent Terrorism and the Western News Media* (London: Sage Publications, 1982).

Schur, Edwin M., *The Politics of Deviance: Stigma Contests and the Uses of Power* (Englewood Cliffs, NJ: Prentice Hall, 1980).

Scott, Marvin B. and Lyman, Stanford M., 'Accounts', *American Sociological Review* 33/1 (February 1968), pp. 46–62.

Scott, Robert A., 'A Proposed Framework for Analyzing Deviance as a Property of Social Order', in Robert A. Scott and Jack Douglas (eds), *Theoretical Perspectives on Deviance* (New York: Basic Books, 1972), pp. 9–35.

Segal, Haggai, *Dear Brothers* (Jerusalem: Keter, 1987; in Hebrew).

Segev, Tom, *The Seventh Million: The Israelis and the Holocaust* (New York: Hill & Wang, 1993).
Shamir, Michal and Arian, Asher, 'The Ethnic Vote in Israel's 1981 Elections', in Asher Arian (ed.), *The Elections in Israel 1981* (Tel Aviv: Ramot, 1983), pp. 91–111.
Shapira, Anita, *Land and Power: The Zionist Resort to Force 1881–1948* (New York: Oxford University Press, 1992).
Smith, Philip, 'Codes and Conflict: Toward a Theory of War as Ritual', *Theory and Society* 20/1 (February 1991), pp. 103–38.
Smith, Philip, 'Civil Society and Violence: Narrative Forms and the Regulation of Social Conflict', in Jennifer Turpin and Lester R. Kurtz (eds), *The Web of Violence: From Interpersonal to Global* (Urbana, IL: University of Illinois Press, 1997), pp. 91–116.
Sontag, Susan, *Illness as Metaphor* (New York: Vintage Books, 1979).
Sprinzak, Ehud, *Every Man Whatsoever is Right in His Own Eyes: Illegalism in Israeli Society* (Tel Aviv: Sifriat Hapoalim, 1986; in Hebrew).
Sprinzak, Ehud, *Political Violence in Israel* (Jerusalem: Jerusalem Institute for Israel Studies 1995; in Hebrew).
Sprinzak, Ehud, *Brother Against Brother: Violence and Extremism in Israeli Politics from Altalena to the Rabin Assassination* (New York: Free Press, 1999).
Sykes, Gresham M. and Matza, David, 'Techniques of Neutralization: A Theory of Delinquency', *American Sociological Review* 22/6 (December 1957), pp. 664–70.
Teveth, Shabtai, *The Arlosoroff Murder* (Jerusalem: Schocken, 1982; in Hebrew).
Thornton, Thomas Perry, 'Terror as a Weapon of Political Agitation', in Harry Eckstein (ed.), *Internal War: Problems and Approaches* (New York: Free Press of Glencoe, 1964), pp. 71–99.
Tololyan, Khachig, 'Cultural Narrative and the Motivation of the Terrorist', *Journal of Strategic Studies* 10/4 (December 1987), pp. 217–33.
Tololyan, Khachig, 'Martyrdom as Legitimacy: Terrorism, Religion and Symbolic Appropriation in the American Diaspora', in Paul Wilkinson and Alasdair M. Stewart (eds), *Contemporary Research in Terrorism* (Aberdeen: Aberdeen University Press, 1987), pp. 89–103.
Tugwell, Maurice A.J., 'Guilt Transfer', in David C. Rapoport and Yonah Alexander (eds), *The Morality of Terrorism: Religious and Secular Justifications* (New York: Pergamon Press, 1982), pp. 275–89.

Verba, Sidney, 'The Kennedy Assassination and the Nature of Political Commitment', in Bradley S. Greenberg and Edwin B. Parker (eds), *The Kennedy Assassination and the American Public: Social Communication in Crisis* (Stanford, CA: Stanford University Press, 1965), pp. 348–60.

Weizmann, Ezer, *The Battle for Peace* (New York: Bantam Books, 1994).

Yadlin, Aharon 'A Just War. Was It Also Unpreventable?', in *The Political–Military Arena: An Examination and Critique of the War in Lebanon* (Ramat Efal: Yad Tabenkin, 1982; in Hebrew), pp. 38–42.

Yariv, Aharon, *War By Choice* (Tel Aviv: Hakibbutz Hameuchad, 1985; in Hebrew).

Yehoshua, A.B., *Between Right and Right. Israel: Problem or Solution?* (Garden City, NY: Doubleday, 1981).

Yerushalmi, Yosef Hayim, *Zakhor: Jewish History, Jewish Memory* (Seattle, WA: University of Washington Press, 1982).

Young, Jock, 'Mass Media, Drugs and Deviance', in Paul Rock and Mary McIntosh (eds), *Deviance and Social Control* (London: Tavistock Publications, 1974), pp. 229–59.

Yurman, Ada, 'The Social Reaction to the Wadi Salib Riots 1959' (unpublished MA thesis, Bar Ilan University, Ramat Gan, 1994; in Hebrew).

Zelizer, Barbie, 'Reading the Past Against the Grain: The Shape of Memory Studies', *Critical Studies in Mass Communication* 12/2 (June 1995), pp. 214–39.

Zerubavel, Yael, *Recovered Roots: Collective Memory and the Making of Israeli National Tradition* (Chicago, IL: University of Chicago Press, 1985).

Index

Abramov, Zalman 20
Adar, Benko 53
Adwan, Kmal 30
Aelia Capitolina (city of Idolatry) 110
agitational and enforcement terror 6
Agudat Yisrael 18, 22, 84, 97
Ahimeir, Aba 118
Al Hamishmar (Mapam daily) 53, 65, 69, 70, 73, 75
Al Nakba (holocaust) 32
Al-Moughrabi, Dalal 30
Alignment; Begin 68, 77–9; elections 63, 65, 67–8, 83; Jordan Valley settlements 19; Likud 67–8, 70, 79–83; map of violence 78; Mapai 15; Nazi analogies 73; partisan action 71; Peres 17; property attacks 66, 79–80, 85–6; violence 68–9, 78; Western Jews 63; Yom Kippur War 17
Almog, Shmuel 106
animality 2, 67, 97–8
anti-assimilation bill 94–5
anti-Peace Now demonstrations 65, 66
anti-war movements 57–8
Arab states 26
Arabs 26–8, 74–5, 91, 92, 97–8, 99
Arafat, Yasser 26, 40, 49, 117
Aretxaga, Begona 8
Argov, Shlomo 44
Ariel, Rav Israel 58–9
Arlosoroff, Chaim 118–21, 123–4, 128
Ashafists 69
Ashkenazi Jews 23
Assad, President 26, 49
assimilation prevention 90–1, 94–5

auxiliaries to violence 85
Avrushmi, Yona 80–1

Balaam 72
banalization of the Holocaust 116–17
Bar Kochba rebellion 108–11, 123
Bar Kochba syndrome 107–11
barbarian references 2, 66–7
Basic Law 96
Begin, Menachem; Arlosoroff murder 119–21; armistice border with Jordan 19; Bar Kochba 110–11; coastal highway raid 38–9, 115; defeat of terrorism promise 41; Deir Yassin force 38–9; demagoguery 69–70, 72, 77, 80; freedom of dissent debate 57; German reparations rally 72–3; Herut 16; Holocaust banalization 116–17; indictment demand 53–4; Israeli–Egyptian peace treaty 19, 20, 114; King of Israel 67, 69–70; left opposition 59; Litani operation 39, 60; mandatory period 38; Nazi analogies 114–15; Palestinian terrorists 97; Peres 47; Phalangists 51; PLO–Nazi analogies 115; Prime Minister 17; Revisionist Zionism 121–2; undiplomatic comments 71–2; violence responsibility 68, 74, 129; War for the Peace of Galilee 44, 46, 51; wars of choice 46–7; West Bank 19–20
Beginism 73
Beirut 44, 45, 51–2, 115
Ben-Ami, Shlomo 75

Ben-Gurion, David 16, 19, 72, 118–19, 121, 129
Ben-Yehuda, Nachman 133
Berger, Peter L. 11, 130–1, 133
Betar youth movement 112
Bialik, Chaim Nachman 40
Black September 44
blood libel 55, 56, 80–1, 118–21
B'nei Akiva youth movement 102
Book of Proverbs 84
borders, defensible 19
boundaries and deviance 135
British 115, 121, 129
British mandate 38, 109

Camp David Accords 20, 21, 27, 49, 113–14, 118
Central Elections Committee 96
centre and periphery image 128–30
centrist party (Shinui) 74
Chief Rabbinate 98
Citizens' Rights Movement 97
civil disobedience 98
civil religion 22
class and voting preferences 63
cleavage lines 132–4
coastal highway operation 26–7, 28–34, 38–9; see also Deir Yassin force; freedom of dissent; Lebanon; Litani Operation
Cohen, Geula 81–2
commission sins 4, 28–34
communist party (Maki) 16
consequences; doctrine of horrible 7; unforeseen 7, 102–3
contrast principle 3–4, 8
corrupted–corrupter model 85–6
Council of Jewish Settlements in Judea, Samaria and Gaza 101
crime control vigilantism 4
criminalization, non-state political violence 2
crowds 2–3, 66
cultural diffusion, secularization as 84
cultures, irreconcilable 75, 76

dangerous violence drift 98
Davar daily 45, 65, 68, 73, 98–9
David and Goliath 32
De-Hahn, Isaac 130
de-Zionization 110

Declaration of Human Rights 46
defensible borders 19
defensive democracy 95
defensive war 46
dehumanization 2–3, 53, 66–7
Deir Yassin force 26, 29–30, 41, 44, 52; see also coastal highway operation; Lebanon; Litani Operation
Dekel, Michael 99
delegitimation 2–3, 8, 86
demagoguery 69–70, 72, 77, 80
democracy 18–19, 95
Democratic Movement for Change (DMC) 17–18
demographic trends, Israeli Jews 91
demonization 69
denial of the victim 30
denigration of victims of violence 85
desecration of God's name (Hillul Hashem) 92
desensitization to violence 83–4
destruction of the Temples 107, 116
deviance 133, 135
deviantization 135
deviants, political 2
diaspora 47, 90
diffusion of culture 84
dissent, freedom of debate 55–8, 59–60
dissidents narratives 8–9, 10
DMC see Democratic Movement for Change
doctrine of horrible consequences 7
Dome of the Rock 27, 36, 38
dominance in body politic 15–18
Draper, Morris 54
Duverger, Maurice 15

Eban, Abba 56–8
education 82, 102, 116
Egypt; exodus myth 33–4; peace treaty 20, 90, 114; Sadat 26, 27
Eitan, Michael 94
Eitan, Rafael 40, 52, 54, 55, 97–8
el-Wazzan, Shaffik 54
Eldad, Israel 109, 110
elections; 1981 63–86, 98; 1984 89, 98; 1988 100
Emigration Fund for Peace 91
enemy; recharacterization 4–5; support for 81
enforcement terror 6

enlightened occupation 75
Eretz Yisrael (Land of Israel) 19, 21, 110
Erikson, Kai 135
Esau, hands of 65–7
Eshkol, Levi 17
can the Ethiopian change his skin? 71–4
ethnic background, voting preferences 63
ethnic divisions without 23; *see also* racism
etiology of violence stories 54, 85–6
Etzel (Irgun Zva Leumi/National Military Organization) 38, 121–4
Etzion, Yehuda 34, 36–7, 38
European Jewry 107, 114–15
Evron, Boaz 117
exodus from Egypt myth 33–4
expulsion of Arabs proposals 92, 99

fascists *see* Nazi analogies
fedayeen 29
Fighters for the Establishment of the State of Israel 122
Fighters for the Freedom of Israel *see* Lehi
the fighting family 121–3
First Temple destruction 116
FLN *see* Front de la Liberation National
force and violence 5–6
foreign affairs 20–1, 72
freedom of dissent debate 55–8, 59–60
Front de la Liberation National (FLN) 116

Gahal 16–17, 23
Galilee *see* War for the Peace of
Gaza 20, 27, 31, 98–9, 101
General Federation of Labor (Histadrut) 45
Geneva Convention 1948 32
gentiles 52, 55, 90–2, 94–5
German reparations demonstration 72–3
Gertz, Nurith 55
Giscard d'Estaing, Valéry 71
government–state identification 69
Greater Israel 21, 27, 69, 70, 98, 113
Green Line 20, 75, 77, 90, 113

Greenzweig, Emil; Alignment 68; Avrushmi arrest 80–1; condemnation in schools 82; historical parallels 73–4; killing 65–7; Peace Now 71, 76; political capital from death 84
guilt transfer 4
Gush Emunim settler movement 19–21, 27, 98, 99, 113

Ha'aretz daily 74, 82
Hacham, Chaim 82
Hadashot daily 94
Ha'ezni, Elyakim 81
Haganah 112–13, 121–2, 123, 130
Hamodia (Agudat Yisrael) 97
Haredi Jews 83–4, 85, 97, 130
Hareven, Shulamit 64–5, 76
Harkabi, Yehoshafat 99, 107–8, 109
Hashomer (The Watchman) 112–13
haters of Israel 56
hatred, groundless 83
Hatzofe (NRP official organ) 100–1
Hausner, Gideon 94
Hebrew; the New 111–14; speaking beautiful 81–2
Hebron 27–8, 35
Heil Kahane 92–6; *see also* Kahane
heroism 41, 74, 112–13, 116
Hersogar, Michael 75
Herut party 16, 19, 23
Herzog, Chaim 39
Herzog, President 93, 97
Hillul Hashem (desecration of God's name) 92
Histadrut (General Federation of Labor) 45
History; the fighting family 121–3; lessons of the past 123–4; and nationalism 106–7; uses of 8–10, 35, 73–4, 120–1; violence past and present 106–7; wars of choice defense 47; *see also* Holocaust; myths; Nazi analogies
Hitler, Adolf 115, 117
Holocaust; banalization 116–17; Israeli–Egyptian peace treaty 114; Kahanism 93; PLO appropriation 41; Remembrance Day 116; State Education Law 116; State of Israel 32; symbolism 107

homa umigdal (tower and stockade settlements) 113
homogeneity of body politic 132
hooligans 67, 77, 82
Horowitz, Dan 23
Hussein, King 44, 49

Ideology; non-state violence 1–2; political 63; re-ideologization 19, 128; return 18–21; vigilantism 27–8; voting preferences 63
IDF *see* Israeli Defence Force
Images; centre and periphery 128–30; perpetrators of violence 66; soul of the land 76–7; vacuum 84; *see also* demagoguery; rhetorics
immigrants, North African and Asian origin 84
implicatory denial 6
incitement to racism 96, 98
incitement to violence 68–9, 70
indictment demands 53–4
insurgent and repressive terror 6
Interim Force in Lebanon (UNIFIL) 27
intermarriage 90, 94
interpretive denial 6
IRA *see* Irish Republican Army
Iran 73, 81
Irgun Zva Leumi *see* Etzel
Irish Republican Army (IRA) 8, 116
Israeli Army *see* Israeli Defence Force
Israeli Defence Force (IDF); anti-war reservists 57; Beirut 51–2; ends and means 48; government defence of 59–60; Israeli Army 45; Litani Operation 26–7, 31, 39, 52; moral standards claim 48; Rabin on role of 45
Israeli Right 98, 100–2
Israeli–Egyptian peace treaty 20, 90, 114

Jabotinsky, Ze'ev 89, 118–19
Jacob, voice of 67–71
Jemayael, Bashir 51
Jerusalem 58, 110, 114
Jerusalem Post 98
Jewish law 91
Jewish myths 32, 33–4
Jewish Underground 27–8, 34–8, 40, 41, 123

Jews; of Eastern (North African or Asian) origin 23, 63, 84; European Jewry 107, 114–15; gentiles dichotomy 55; and terrorism 26–8; Western 23, 63
Jordan 44
Jordan Valley settlements 19
Judea 19, 111
jus ad bellum 47–8, 59
jus in belli 48, 59

Kach Party 89, 92–3, 96, 99, 101
Kahan Report 64, 68, 83
Kahane, Meir 10, 89–103
Kahanism 93
Kahanization process 99
Khomeini, Ayatollah 73
Khomeinists label 81
Kiba massacre 52
Kimmerling (Baruch) 102
Kissinger, Henry 72
Knesset House Committee 94
Knesset parties composition 14
Kook, Rav Avraham 41
Kotler, Yair 92–3

labelling process 1
Labour; Camp David Accords 113–14; Kahane 97–8; Mapai 15; political camp 14; street violence 81; Trumpeldor 112; wars of choice 47–8, 60; Zionist historiography 107
Labour Zionism 18–19, 22, 112, 118, 122
Land of Israel (Eretz Yisrael) 19, 110
last resort strategy 6, 28
law and order 7, 85
Le Bon, Gustave 2–3
League of Nations 121
Lebanon; invasions 39–40, 49–51, 56–9, 60, 109; PLO in 44; PLO-free zone 49; UNIFIL 27; *see also* coastal highway operation; freedom of dissent; Litani Operation; War for the Peace of Galilee
Leeman, Richard 6–7
left; opposition to Begin 59; prior violence and Peace Now 81; reactions to Kahane 103

legitimation; by history 107; delegitimation 2, 8, 86; Labour Zionism 22; Likud 70; of the present 123–4; Revisionist Zionism 121; self-legitimation 134–5
Lehi (Lohamei Herut Yisrael/Fighters for the Freedom of Israel) 38, 121, 122–4
lessons of the past 123–4
Levin, Hanoch 118
Levinger, Rabbi 99
lexicon of incitement 68–9
liberated territories debate 19
Likud; Agudat Yisrael 18; Alignment 76, 79–83; Begin 16, 79–80; Camp David Accords 21; deviantization 135; ethnic patterns 23; historiography 107; Jewish dimensions of Israeli society 21–2; Jewish Underground 34–5, 38, 40; Jews of Eastern origin 23, 63; joint committee proposal 70; Lebanon invasion 39–40, 60; mandatory period 38; map of violence 78; multi-cleavage society 23; NRP alliance 22; occupied territory 75; PLO 40; repolarization 102; right-wing ascendancy 98; settlements 19–20, 77; stigma contests 128–9; West Bank policy 19–20; *see also* elections
lines of cleavage 132–4
Lissak, Moshe 23
Litani Operation 26–7, 31–2, 39, 44, 52; *see also* coastal highway operation; Deir Yassin force; freedom of dissent; Lebanon
literal denial 6
Lohamei Herut Yisrael *see* Lehi
Lorenz, Shlomo 84
Luckmann, Thomas 11, 130–1, 133

Maki (Israeli Communist Party) 16
map of violence 78
Mapai dominance 15–16
Mapam daily (*Al Hamishmar*) 53, 65, 69, 70, 73, 75
Margalit, Avishai 99
martyrologies 9
martyrs in a holy war (*shahidim*) 29, 30
massacres 51–5

Matza, David 30
mayors, West Bank 27, 74–5
medical analogies 2, 84
Megged, Aharon 93
Meir, Golda 17
messianic process 38
Michael, B. 100
millenarian terrorists 36
millenarianism 37
Milo, Ronnie 82
Moledet Party 100
moral justifications 3
moral panics 129
morality plays 40–1
Morasha party 98
Moses, Noah 93
Movement for a Greater Israel 113
Movement to Halt the Retreat in Sinai 27
Munich agreement 118
Muslims, Temple Mount 36–7
myths; exodus 33–4; expansionism 113–14; Palestinian appropriation of Jewish 32, 33–4; Tel Hai 113; of unrealism 108–9; *see also* stories

narratives 8–10; *see also* myths; stories
national chauvinism 73
National Liberation Front *see* Front de la Liberation National
National Military Organization *see* Etzel
National Religious Party (NRP) 18, 20–2, 38, 98, 100–1
national self-reckoning 108
National Unity government 16–17, 89, 97
nationalism and history 106–7
nationalist narratives 9
natural science analogies 84
Navon, President 54
Nazi analogies; Begin 47, 114–15; election campaign 73–4; Kahane 93–5; Likud 81; PLO 32–3, 38–9
Ne'eman, Yuval 58
Nekuda journal 101
neutrality stance, PLO 26
neutralization policy 91
never again 114–18
the New Hebrew 111–14
nihilation strategy 131, 133, 135
Nir, Shaul 35

no-choice wars 45–6, 47
non-homogeneity of body politic 132
non-Jews restrictions 90–1
non-state violence 1–4, 5, 134–5
NRP *see* National Religious Party
Nuremberg Laws 94

occupation, enlightened 75
occupied territories 19, 74, 97–8
omission sins 4, 34–7
opposition duty 57
organic metaphors 84
Oz, Amos 76–7

Palestine, Camp David Accords 27
Palestine Liberation Organization (PLO); Begin on 115; Black September 44; coastal highway raid 26, 28–34, 41, 115; exodus from Egypt myth 33–4; Holocaust 41; IRA comparison 116; Jordan 44; Lebanon 44, 49; Likud 40; Litani Operation 39; Nazi comparisons 38–9, 115; neutrality stance 26; non-intervention in Arab states policy 26; PLO–free zone 49; racism 93; righteous determination 29; strategy of last resort 28; victimization rhetoric 31, 33–4, 41; violence justification 28–34; War for the Peace of Galilee 20
Palestine National Guidance Committee 27
Palestine Perspectives 30
Palestinian Passover 33–4
Palestinian state 19, 20, 49
Partition 19, 121
Passover 33–4
past; lessons of 123–4; and present violence 106–7
patriotism 74
Peace Now 64–5, 71, 76, 81, 99; *see also* anti-Peace Now demonstrations
Peel Commission 19
Penal Law 96
Peres, Shimon; Alignment 17; assault 79, 81; Begin 47, 73; Beirut 51–2; ends and means 48; Greenzweig killing 68; invasion of Lebanon 55–6; Kahane 103; Sabra and Shatilla 51–2
periphery 128–30

perpetrators of violence images 66
Phalangists 51, 52, 53–4
PLO *see* Palestine Liberation Organization
poisoners of wells 55–8
political deviants, delegitimation 2
political ideology, voting preferences 63
present legitimation 123–4
Psychology; crowd 66; of dissent 56

Rabin, Yitzhak 17, 45, 46
racial incitement 96, 98
racism 89–90, 93, 96, 97–100, 102–3, 117; *see also* Kahane
radicalization of Israeli Right 100–2
Ravitsky, Aviezer 90
re-ideologization 19, 128
reality; constructions 130–1; unrealism 108–9
recharacterization of the enemy 4–5
redemption theology 21, 27, 38, 91–2
reflective strategy 6–7
refugee camps massacre 51–5
religion and voting preferences 63
religious political camp 14, 18, 21
religious right 21, 54, 58–9, 98, 101
Remembrance Day 116
'Reply to Menachem Begin' (Peres) 47
resident stranger status 91
residential restrictions 94
return of ideology 18–21
revenge 39
Revisionist Zionism 19, 107, 110, 121–2, 128
Revisionists 14, 22, 75, 118–19, 120
rhetorics 8, 31, 33–4, 41, 85–6; *see also* demagoguery; images
Riches, David 6
right; long journey to the 97–100; religious 21, 54, 58–9, 98, 101
Rogel, Nakdimon 112
Roman Empire 108–11, 129
Rosenblatt, Zvi 118
Rubinstein, Danny 98

Sabra and Shatilla refugee camp massacre 51–5
sacred and profane distinction 5
Sadat, President 26, 27
Samaria 19, 101
Sarid, Yossi 56, 70, 75, 97, 101

INDEX

Savidor, Menachem 82
Schiff, Ze'ev 51
Schmidt, Helmut 71
Schur, Edwin 7, 132–3
scorched-earth policy 31
Second Temple destruction 107, 116
secular Zionism 83, 84, 97, 130, 132
secularization 84
self-defence right 45, 46
self-legitimation 134–5
self-reckoning, national 108
semantic strategies 6
Sephardi Jews 23
settlements; inducements 19–20; Jordan Valley 19; map 77; Tel Hai 111–12; tower and stockade 113; *see also* Green Line
settlers; Camp David Accords–Munich agreement comparison 118; Gush Emunim 19–21, 27, 98, 99, 113; Jewish state survival 90; Trumpeldor 111, 113, 123; violence against Arabs 74–5
shahidim (martyrs in a holy war) 29, 30
shame barrier 99
Shamir, Yitzhak 38
Shapira, Yosef 99
Sharon, Ariel; dismissal 64; freedom of dissent debate 55; indictment demand 53–4; Kahan Report 68; left opposition 59; massacres response 54; Peace Now rally 64–5; Phalangists 51; War for the Peace of Galilee 44–5
Shiloah, Zvi 113
Shinui (centrist) party 74
Sinai 20, 27, 47–8, 90, 113–14
sins; of commission 4, 28–34; of omission 34–7
Six Day War 47, 90, 108
slippery slope argument 7
Sobol, Yehoshua 71
social constructionism 1, 130–1
socialist Zionism 15–16
'A Song for a Palestinian Passover' 33–4
soul of the land image 76–7
South Lebanon, PLO-free zone 49
Soviet Union 115, 116
spilling the blood 74–5

state; historical narratives 9–10; state-centred paradigm 1, 134; and violence 5–8
State Education Law 116
State of Israel; Bar Kochba Rebellion 109, 110; Camp David Accords 27; government identification 69; Holocaust 32; IDF role 45; millenarian arguments 37; nationalism and history 106–7; PLO destruction allegation 40
Stavsky, Abraham 118
Steadfastness and Confrontation Front 26
Stern, Avraham (Yair) 122
stigma contests; contexts 14; governments 10–11, 135; Kahane election 89; law and order 7; Likud period 128–9; morality plays rhetoric 41; non-state actors 5
stories; etiological 54, 85–6; *see also* myths; narratives
strategy of last resort 6, 28
street violence *see* violence on the streets
Sykes, Gresham M. 30
symbolic universes 11, 130–2
symbolism of the Holocaust 107
Syria 49, 50

tales of violence 8–10
Techiya party 21, 81–2, 98, 113
Tel Aviv 26
Tel Hai 107, 111–13
Temple Institute 58
Temple Mount 36–7
Temples destruction 107, 116
territorial democracy 18–19
territories for peace 21
terrorism; Arabs and Jews 26–8; delegitimation 2–3; morality plays 40–1; sinner or sinned against 38–40; sins of commission 28–34; sins of omission 34–7; types 6; use of term 31–2
theology, redemption 21, 27, 38, 91–2
Tololyan, Khachig 9
Torah 58, 59, 84, 85, 101
tower and stockade settlements 113
transfer; Arab populations 99; of guilt 4
Trumpeldor, Yosef 111, 113, 123
Tugwell, Maurice 4

ultra-orthodox Judaism 83, 84, 129–30; see also Haredi
unforeseen consequences 7, 102–3
United Nations (UN) 27, 32, 46; Interim Force in Lebanon (UNIFIL) 27
United States (US) 36, 84, 97
universe; maintenance 131, 132–3; symbolic 11, 130–2
unrealism myths 108–9
the upheaval 14
US see United States
uses of history 8–10, 35, 73–4, 120–1

vacuum image 84
Verba, Sidney 86
verbal violence; physical violence relation 82; street violence relation 71–2
victims; denial of 30; denigration 85
vigilantism 4, 27–8, 35–8
violence; auxiliaries 85; crowd psychology 66; force 5–6; non-state 1–4, 134–5; secular Zionism 130; on the streets 63–5, 74, 122–3, 130; verbal 71–2, 82
Virshuvsky, Mordechai 74
visions of Zionism 19, 76, 133
voting preferences 63

Waqf control of Temple Mount 36
War of Attrition 47
War of Independence 47, 109, 122
War for the Peace of Galilee 20, 44–5, 49–50, 51
wars; of choice 20, 44–51, 60; defensive 46; *jus ad bellum* 47–8, 59; *jus in belli* 48, 59; no-choice 45–6, 47
The Watchman 112–13

Weber, Max 1, 5
Weinberger, Casper 72
Weiss, Daniella 99
Weizmann, Ezer 34–5, 40
West Bank 19–20, 31, 98; mayors murder 27, 74–5
Western Jews 23, 63; see also European Jewry
World Zionist Organization 18

Ya'ari, Ehud 51
Yadin, Yigal 17, 109, 110
Yadlin, Aharon 50
Yamit 74, 98
Yediot Achronot daily 56, 93
Yehoshua, A.B. 117
Yishuv; Arlosoroff murder 118–19, 120; Etzel 121; ideology 18–19; Lehi 121; Mapai 15–16; Revisionism 75; Revisionist Zionism 128; Tel Hai 111, 112–13
Yizhar, S. 45–6, 53, 76
Yom Kippur War 17, 22, 47, 72
Young Guard faction 20
Young, Jock 2
youth movements 102, 112

Zamir, Yitzhak 93
Ze'evi, Rechavam 100
Zionism; de-Zionization 110; expansionism 113–14; historiography 106–7; Holocaust 32; or hooliganism 77; Jewish majority 91; Jewish Underground 41; Kahane 10; Labour Zionism 18–19, 22, 112, 118, 122; Revisionist 19; secular 83, 84, 97; socialist 15–16; Tel Hai 111–12; visions 19, 76, 133

For Product Safety Concerns and Information please contact our EU
representative GPSR@taylorandfrancis.com
Taylor & Francis Verlag GmbH, Kaufingerstraße 24, 80331 München, Germany

www.ingramcontent.com/pod-product-compliance
Lightning Source LLC
Chambersburg PA
CBHW051102230426
43667CB00013B/2402